Escaping
Jurassic
Government

Escaping Jurassic Government

HOW TO RECOVER AMERICA'S LOST COMMITMENT TO COMPETENCE

Donald F. Kettl

BROOKINGS INSTITUTION PRESS
Washington, D.C.

The Brookings Institution is a private nonprofit organization devoted to research, education, and publication on important issues of domestic and foreign policy. Its principal purpose is to bring the highest quality independent research and analysis to bear on current and emerging policy problems. Interpretations or conclusions in Brookings publications should be understood to be solely those of the authors.

Library of Congress Cataloging-in-Publication data

Names: Kettl, Donald F., author.
Title: Escaping jurassic government : how to recover America's lost commitment to competence / Donald F. Kettl.
Description: Washington, D.C. : Brookings Institution Press, 2016. | Description based on print version record and CIP data provided by publisher; resource not viewed.
Identifiers: LCCN 2015051473 (print) | LCCN 2015040127 (ebook) | ISBN 9780815728023 (epub) | ISBN 9780815728115 (pdf) | ISBN 9780815728016 (paperback)
Subjects: LCSH: Public administration—United States. | Administrative Agencies—United States—Management. | Government accountability— United States. | Transparency in government—United States. | Government Productivity—United States. | Organizational effectiveness—United States. | BISAC: POLITICAL SCIENCE / Government / National. | POLITICAL SCIENCE / Government / Legislative Branch. | POLITICAL SCIENCE / Public Policy / Social Policy.
Classification: LCC JK421 (print) | LCC JK421 .K478 2016 (ebook) | DDC 351.73—dc23
LC record available at http://lccn.loc.gov/2015051473

9 8 7 6 5 4 3 2 1

Typeset in Janson Text LT Std Roman

Composition by Westchester Publishing Services

To John J. DiIulio Jr.
An unmatched intellectual, a gifted public servant,
and a wonderful friend

Contents

Preface

THERE IS A LARGE AND growing gap in American government, between what people expect government to do and what government can actually accomplish. Citizens look at what the private sector does, from overnight delivery of products purchased with a single click to one-stop online access to their finances, and they wonder why government cannot do as well. For the public sector, there's the endless parade of media tales about government failures. Inside Internet echo chambers, social media reinforces a cynical and sometimes even nasty view of government. Candidates for office have not only discovered they can make hay out of attacking Washington, but they have increasingly suggested that the policy game has been captured by a professional political class, which has rigged the system to benefit insiders while freezing out ordinary citizens.

It's not just cynics, reporters, and social media ideologues who wonder about government failures. In a sweeping critique of American government, Francis Fukuyama has argued that the rising power of special interests has trapped the system in political decay.¹ Thomas E. Mann and Norman J. Ornstein have sadly concluded, "It's even worse than it looks."² The gap has widened between citizens' expectations and government's performance. There's also an underlying sense that citizens have become walled off from the government they're taxed to provide.

Some of this, of course, is the product of citizens' rising—and sometimes impossible—expectations about what government ought to do for them. No matter the issue, the first instinct when problems arise, even among the biggest advocates of the smallest government, is to see government as the cavalry and wonder why it doesn't arrive faster to help save the day. There's virtually no problem that citizens don't call on government to solve, from flooded basements and giant sinkholes to help after epic natural disasters and protection from lone-wolf terrorists. Almost no one likes big government, but no one expects to have to cope with problems alone.

And that's laid the foundation for the biggest challenge for American government in the 21st century. As 18th-century French philosopher Jean-Jacques Rousseau contended, government is based on a social contract with its citizens. The combination of the rising expectations about what government should do and the manifest challenges in meeting those expectations has frayed, perhaps even fractured, that contract. So, too, has the growing sense that government is in business to help those hard-wired into its operations, at the expense of citizens locked outside. When it comes to government, especially at the federal level, there are growing worries about what is possible but no lack of challenges to attack.

Figuring out how we got to this place is the goal of this book. It begins with a simple premise. Modern American government grew from a core belief, supported by both Republicans and Democrats, that emerged with the Progressives in the late 19th century: whatever government chose to do, it had a responsibility to do it well. In the last decades of the 20th century, however, conflict over government's mission increased—and the shared commitment to competence eroded. We continued to ask more of government, from ending poverty and eliminating pollution to defending the homeland and protecting the financial system. We became increasingly enraptured by the notion that the private sector could do anything we wanted to do better than government could do it. We lost trust in government and its ability to perform. So, to work through these dilemmas, we relied ever more on strategies that have interwoven government's role into the private and nonprofit sectors. Government increasingly is everywhere, because we want it to do more. But we've worked hard to undermine its capacity and to wipe away its fingerprints, because we don't trust government to do it.

As I explain in the book, these trends have, in many cases, eliminated the line of sight between citizens and what their government does for them. In turn, this has unraveled the social contract, because the parties have increasingly lost the connection with each other. Moreover, as government has invented new tools to meet citizens' impossible expectation of more help without more government, it has not invented the skills needed to use these tools well. That has eroded trust in government's ability to perform.

Half of the book focuses on explaining how we got here; the other half lays out a hopeful theory about how we can crack this nut. It arrays four scenarios through which government can evolve in the coming decades. One seems both most likely and most positive: a government that develops new skills, through powerful new data tools and better managers to use them, to leverage the partners on which it relies to serve the public. We have proven we can make this model work, but the consequences if we do not are dire. The dinosaurs went extinct because they failed to adapt, and the same could happen to American government. But, like Ebenezer Scrooge's vision of the ghost of Christmas yet to come, this represents a future that *may* occur—but which need not occur, if we have our civic wits about us. We have it in our power to write a fresh draft of the social contract for the 21st century, if we put our minds to recovering the nation's lost commitment to competence. That, I conclude, is the key to escaping the Jurassic government that plagues us, a government that has increasingly fallen out of sync with its environment.

This book grew out of conversations with Jonathan Breul, a smart and keen observer of American management and politics from his many years of service in the U.S. Office of Management and Budget. He challenged me to think about government's future and the forces most likely to shape it. Our conversations proved enormously helpful, not only in thinking about how to peer into the crystal ball but also in identifying the big issues most likely to shape that vision. I'm especially grateful to him for suggesting how to stay firmly grounded in current reality while looking aggressively forward. I'm grateful as well for the comments and suggestions of three reviewers for Brookings, who helped immeasurably to improve the final product.

I'm especially grateful as well to John J. DiIulio Jr., who has proven to be one of America's most important and enduring public intellectuals. He brings to every puzzle a remarkable sweep of history, an unmatched insight into the interplay of politics and management, and the instinct for effective action that can only come from service at the top levels of government. He has been a gentle critic and an exceptionally good friend, in this project and in many others across the years. I count myself lucky indeed to have had the enormous benefit of such a keenly shrewd sage. He has fueled my energy to try to solve the puzzles of public affairs, and he has been an uncommon model on how best to do it.

Finally, this project—like everything else good in my life over the last 40 years—would not have been possible without the love and support of my wife, Sue. She's been the best friend and companion that anyone could want, through countless adventures, and my thanks here are only a shadow of what she deserves.

ONE

Failure to Adapt

THERE ARE MANY THINGS WE do not know about the Jurassic period, when dinosaurs ruled the earth. But one thing is certain: Dinosaurs went extinct because they failed to adapt. It might have been because the atmosphere became clogged with debris from an asteroid that hit the earth. It could have been the result of massive volcanic eruptions. Although scientists rate the blue whale as the largest creature that has ever lived, dinosaurs as a class rank as the most powerful and fearsome creatures that have roamed the planet. But strength and longevity are no guarantees of durability and endurance. Dinosaurs disappeared when they could not cope with change that wiped out what they needed to live on, even though starfish, turtles, and salamanders survived.

Nothing that gets out of sync with its environment lasts long—and that goes for governments just as much as dinosaurs. There are already warning signs that American government has late-Jurassic-period challenges. Like the dinosaurs, government is strong and powerful. But like the forces that led the dinosaurs to extinction, government is failing to adapt to the challenges it faces. American government struggles with its most important and fundamental decisions. Even worse, it too often fails to deliver on the decisions it makes. That wastes scarce public money and leaves citizens disappointed. It's a profoundly serious problem that, if government does not evolve quickly enough, could lead American government down the same path that devastated the Jurassic-age dinosaurs. The book is hopeful, however, for the tools for avoiding this future lie within our grasp. We have the ability to escape Jurassic government, if we recover our government's lost commitment to competence.

It is no secret that American government is in a precarious position. Trust in public institutions is at a historic low. Public distrust in the ability of government to deliver on its promises is high. In far too many areas, government does not perform well. Tight budgets make it hard to launch anything new, and the fiscal pinch is forcing excruciating decisions about what to cut. Oceans of budgetary red ink slosh ahead for as far as we can see. Fed up with government's intrusion in our lives, conservatives pledge to "starve the beast." Liberals struggle mightily to make good on the ambitious promises they have made. Public employees find themselves a handy target for everything that goes wrong, since it is easier to target the instrument than what it seeks to accomplish. There is little satisfaction in the government we have and no consensus on how to make it better.

A thoughtful political scientist from the University of California, Berkeley, Todd La Porte, sadly wonders about a "heightened sense of latent dread," with public problems that are growing larger and government's capacity to solve them shrinking.[1] In fact, an August 2015 poll showed that just 2 percent of Americans were "enthusiastic" about the federal government. Another 21 percent were "satisfied but not enthusiastic." Three-fourths of those surveyed had negative feelings toward the federal government, including 27 percent who were down-right "angry."[2] In yet another poll, taken in July 2015, a third of re-spondents thought that the government was "too big," and 28 percent found it "not transparent." But the biggest problems were that gov-ernment was simply not managed well: It was "inefficient" (73 percent), "wasteful" (63 percent), "out of touch" (63 percent), and "corrupt" (67 percent).[3] There simply is no fixing what ails American government without improving its capacity to deliver on what citizens pay for—and rightly expect to work.

There are explanations aplenty for the sorry state of American de-mocracy, but at the core is a simple fact: We have lost our commit-ment to competence—to a belief that, whatever government leaders decide, they will deliver on their promises. For more than 130 years, from the late 19th century to the early post–World War II years, we built a government consensus on competence. Led by both Republi-cans and Democrats, Progressives established the modern American government. They battled fiercely over *what government ought to do*. But when they reached consensus, there was a bipartisan commitment *to making government work*.

Along the way, however, an insidious fear grew among citizens, fed by their elected leaders, that government was out to ruin the country and that government itself had become the problem. In her 2015 best seller, set in the 1950s, *Go Set a Watchman*, Harper Lee casts a char-acter, Uncle Jack, as a profound cynic of government. "Cynical, hell," he says. "I'm a healthy old man with a constitutional mistrust of paternalism and government in large doses." He goes on, "The only thing I'm afraid of about this country is that its government will some-day become so monstrous that the smallest person living in it will be trampled underfoot, and then it wouldn't be worth living in."[4] Many citizens and their elected officials managed to convince themselves that Uncle Jack's fears had come to dominate government and the country. That allowed Ronald Reagan, in 1986, to win lasting applause from the Right—and grudging respect from the Left—when he said, "The nine most terrifying words in the English language are: I'm from the Government, and I'm here to help."[5]

The contrast with a century before could not have been deeper. The Progressive spirit—a bipartisan dedication not to *big* government but to *effective* government—created the modern American state. It reined in corporate trusts and improved the lives of sweatshop workers. It created the modern executive establishment, from the Federal Reserve to the nation's budgetary and civil service policies. It fought and won two world wars, built interstate highways, and put a man on the moon. It tackled, more or less well, a new era of social and economic problems, from poverty to pollution.

Starting in the 1970s, however, the Progressive tradition gradually drifted out of sync with government's mission, as too many citizens and elected officials alike lost faith in government and its ability to deliver. The tradition took on a reputation for big government at all costs and a partisan leaning toward Democrats, instead of bipartisan commitment to competence. Instead of pursuing a commitment to making government work, it grew into a lack of confidence in government to work at all. As the astute political scientist, John J. DiIulio Jr., observed, we have fallen into a deepening spiral of overreach by Democrats, in launching ambitious programs but failing to build the capacity to manage them, and disinvestment by Republicans, in preaching the virtues of cutting government but failing to ensure that the parts of government they believe in actually work.[6] On one level, this spiral is a natural product of the partisan gridlock that has seized up the nation's political machinery. On a deeper level, it has helped create and feed that gridlock, by allowing the two political parties to follow their very different political ideologies to the same unhappy place: A government that too often fails to deliver, that encourages citizens' cynicism, and that reinforces the ideologies that feed deepening incompetence and latent dread.

But this is not a book about cynicism or pessimism. It has a profoundly positive view of American government and what it can—and must—do for citizens, and it advances that view through a simple argument. We might not like all of what government does, but we are not about to lessen our expectations that it should do it. We might not believe that government can meet these expectations, but it actually does far better, far more often than we think. We can take straightforward steps to help government meet the challenges it faces in the 21st century. And, by doing so, we can reclaim our government and the lost bipartisan promise on which it was built. In the pages that follow, I will explore the challenges that led us to our current predicament and the steps we can take to escape the fate of the Jurassic dinosaurs.

We have been fighting over what government should do as long as there has been a country to fight over. But we need to restore government's capacity to deliver on what we decide as a country we ought to accomplish. That will not magically unlock gridlock, but we do have it within our grasp to restore confidence that what the government seeks to do it will do well. In the turbulent world of gridlocked politics, restoring America's commitment to competence would be no mean feat.

ESCAPING MADISON'S "WRETCHED SITUATION"

In a 1788 speech, James Madison wondered about those we elect to govern. "Is there no virtue among us? If there be not, we are in a wretched situation," he said.[7] It often seems that, over the past century, Madison's worst fears have come true. In that time, the scope and power of government grew enormously, from new entitlement programs like Social Security and Medicare to the vast array of new government agencies. But there was also the simultaneous growth of a bipartisan commitment to competent government, led by the

Progressive spirit. There were fierce battles about just what government ought to do. But once the conflicts settled about the *what*, there was a surprising (to us today, at least) commitment about the *how*: with a professional, not an amateur, government.

Reformers on both sides of the political aisle were alert, of course, to the worries about governmental tyranny that preoccupied the founders and led to Madison's separation of powers. The Progressives developed their own strategy to empower government without unleashing tyranny by building strong boundaries. Some of the boundaries were structural, such as the creation of independent regulatory agencies. Some of the boundaries were procedural, such as a civil service system and a comprehensive executive budget, to constrain arbitrary actions and to put the key decisions in the sunshine for all to see.

Perhaps most important, this Progressive spirit had distinctly bipartisan roots. It did not spring from the roots of big-government liberal Democrats, although that is the meaning the "Progressive" label has acquired over time. In fact, many of the most important Progressive reforms emerged from Republican administrations (see table 1-1), as well as Democratic ones, and these bipartisan roots are the secret sauce that helped the modern administrative state grow and endure. In fact, that is one of the secrets about why the Progressive movement and its imprint on the modern administrative state endured so long. Both parties shared a commitment to "take Care that the Laws be faithfully executed," as the president swears in the oath prescribed in the Constitution, and that that principle guided the expansion of the American state.

However, as government became more muscular during the 20th century, both political parties gradually slid away from that bipartisan consensus. Democrats began focusing more on their policy ambitions than on how to fulfill them. Republicans, unable to repeal many programs, fought rearguard actions to weaken those programs by weakening their execution. As a result, confidence in the Progressives' strategy, including their commitment to a professionalized civil

Table 1-1. The Bipartisan Foundations of the Progressive State

INITIATIVE	PRESIDENT	PARTY	YEAR
Civil Service Reform Act *Advance a professional civil service*	Arthur	Republican	1883
Interstate Commerce Commission *Regulate railroads and trucking* *to reduce monopoly power*	Cleveland	Democrat	1883
Bureau of Internal Revenue (later Internal Revenue Service— Eisenhower [Republican, 1953]) *Collect income taxes*	Cleveland	Democrat	1894
Department of Commerce *Advance the interests of business*	T. Roosevelt	Republican	1903
Food and Drug Administration *Protect safety of food and* *pharmaceuticals*	T. Roosevelt	Republican	1906
Federal Reserve *Manage the supply of money and* *credit*	Wilson	Democrat	1913
Department of Labor *Advance the interests of labor*	Wilson	Democrat	1913
Federal Trade Commission *Prevent unfair business practices,* *especially monopoly power*	Wilson	Democrat	1914
Budget and Accounting Act *Create a comprehensive* *executive budget*	Harding	Republican	1921
Occupational Safety and Health Administration *Regulate the safety of the workplace*	Nixon	Republican	1970
Environmental Protection Agency *Improve the quality of air, water,* *and soil*	Nixon	Republican	1970

service and comprehensive executive budgeting, withered. The bureaucratic boundaries constraining governmental power softened as we came to rely more on nongovernmental proxies to do government's work, beyond the boundaries of the bureaucracy. Most important, the consensus around the Progressives' commitment to effective government melted under the weight of partisanship and gridlock.

This unintended conspiracy, not surprisingly, increased government's performance problems. It was little wonder that the public's confidence in government shrank. There was a growing sense that an ever-larger, often unaccountable, and sometimes evil government had permeated every corner of our lives. In fact, as we see a bit later in the book, government has in fact pervaded virtually every nook and cranny of society, but that was precisely because Americans wanted it that way. But the failure to ensure that a commitment to competence supported that expansion led to ongoing performance problems that, in turn, cracked the Progressives' foundations of professional execution and strong accountability. It then set the stage for the bipartisan conspiracy of blaming government for almost everything.

For more than a century, we fought mainly over the *what* of policy but had a strong consensus about the *how*. We have now moved to a new stage that reverses that balance. Much of the what is largely a settled question, because partisan gridlock and demographic trends already in motion make it hard either to grow or to shrink government. The big policy disputes are largely at the margins. At the same time, the how consensus has evaporated. Indeed, some partisans are trying to halt government's ability to deliver on some promises, and libertarians are trying to dismantle the state. Within both the Republican and Democratic camps, policy strategies have emerged that have led to a neglect of administrative capacity. It has become fashionable to argue that government ought to be run more like the private sector and that, wherever possible, government ought to spin its functions into a vast array of linkages with private proxies, including contracts, quasi-governmental corporations, tax breaks, regulations, and other indirect proxy-based mechanisms. Compared with the Progressives' strategy of a stronger government strongly managed with strong boundaries, these proxy mechanisms are usually harder to manage and hold accountable. More important, they blurred the boundaries of public accountability by interweaving the governmental and nongovernmental worlds, and they have increased the disconnection between citizens and their government. What worked for the era of strong direct government works badly for leveraging nongovernmental proxies.

For more than a century, the system the Progressives built provided the foundation for both Republican and Democratic policies. But as gridlock grew and polarization increased, that consensus dissolved. The partisan debates seem to suggest that the big battles are about *what* government should do and *how big* it should be. These contests are fierce, but the far more fundamental—but often hidden—question we face is how government should do its work. Not only do we not know the answer to that question; all too often we do not even recognize that it has become the central question. Until we figure out new strategies and tactics to do what the people want to do—and insist on doing—and until we understand that this is a critical puzzle, we are doomed to policy gridlock and performance poison.

Over time, the Progressive movement fell out of sync with Progressive policies. No new consensus has emerged to replace it. And without a consensus on how the laws should be faithfully executed, the performance of the nation's policies will inevitably suffer. That is the core of why so many Americans, both ordinary citizens and their elected officials, have lost faith in American government.

The dominant strategies and tactics for the first half of the 20th century gradually became a poor fit for post–World War II American governance. The boundaries have eroded, political support for government professionalism has waned, and both parties found different tactical roads to the same unhappy place: a government without a core commitment to make governance work. We cannot stay where we are without risking government's ability to perform, and we cannot risk government's ability to perform without further undermining confidence in government. Liberals campaigned for a larger governmental portrait without figuring out how government would paint the strokes. Conservatives insisted on a smaller government and campaigned to limit the power of government's bureaucrats without determining how to deliver the government programs that citizens continued to expect. The Progressives' strategy for modern American government has gradually eroded.

What we are left with is a collection of tactical, uneasy compromises made since World War II to hold the basic Progressive strategy together. That is the foundation for the increased interweaving of government with the nongovernmental sectors and among the federal, state, and local levels of government: more government programs managed indirectly through a broader collection of proxy tools. The tactic allowed liberals to grow government without taking account of government's growing size, and it allowed conservatives to accept the growing role of government without accepting its increasing reach. This unspoken conspiracy allowed government to transform with remarkable speed and breadth. As government used these tools more, figuring how to use them effectively and to hold them accountable was an afterthought, if there was any thought at all.

It is little wonder that the result has been a collection of performance problems and deepening distrust of government. This was a direct result of the obsession of ideologues, on all sides, about the what of government, at the expense of the how—until the how questions became increasingly problematic and began undermining government's capacity to perform the what. It did not happen instantly. The roots, in fact, were clear even in the 1960s, when John F. Kennedy noted, "Most of us are conditioned for many years to have a viewpoint, Republican or Democratic—liberal, conservative, moderate." But, he pointed out, most of the problems we face no longer can be sorted into neat ideological bins. Rather, most of the problems we face, he said, "are administrative problems," which require "very sophisticated judgments which do not lend themselves to the great sort of 'passionate moments' which have stirred this country so often in the past."[8] The more we focus on ideological judgments about policy, the more we miss Kennedy's insight that it is in the delivery of our promises that the country's big issues increasingly rest.

In the 21st century, government's role has steadily expanded, despite rhetoric on all sides about hemming it in. A major driver has been government's effort to manage, control, and limit the risks to which citizens are subject. The governmental and nongovernmental sectors have become more interconnected because citizens have called on government increasingly to protect them from harm (like terrorist attacks), to help them recover from adverse events (like hurricanes and tornadoes), and to help insulate them from the often unpredictable behavior of private markets (especially after the 2008 economic collapse). A careful reading of the Constitution does not show this as a fundamental function of government, except perhaps to "promote the general welfare," but the management of risk has become one of the most important foundations for the expansion of government since the late 1800s—and for the interpenetration of the governmental and nongovernmental sectors.

The erosion of the Progressive commitment to competence shows no signs of abating. Even worse, there is no plan, on any front, for fixing the problems into which government's capacity to deliver has fallen. But as government's capacity has fallen out of sync with the challenges it must solve, the public's expectations have scarcely decreased. Even the loudest of small-government advocates expect government to be there when they need it.

Consider the case of the wildfires that savaged central Texas in 2011. Rep. Michael McCaul (R-Tex.), who represented the area, hammered the U.S. Forest Service for failing to pre-position a giant DC-10 aerial tanker so it was ready to fight the outbreak, for allowing the plane to sit on a Texas runway for 48 hours when it did arrive, and then for keeping smaller P-3 Orion tankers on the ground in California when they could have been used to fight the Texas wildfires. Given the enormous damage the fires were causing in Texas, especially around Bastrop, it was easy to understand his frustration that planes were sitting idle as the brush was burning. But the issue proved much more complicated and far more interesting. The DC-10 was not operated by the Forest Service but by a private contractor working for the agency. The crew members of the DC-10 had logged so many flying hours that they were required to rest. (There had been accidents in the past when tired crews pushed themselves past human limits.) The local support team needed to put together a facility to prepare the flame retardant that the plane would drop, so it took time to get the plane ready. As for the P-3 Orion tankers: They were indeed sitting on the ground—because the separate contractor that owned and operated the planes, Aero Union, had not completed the required safety inspections. (In the past, there had been accidents where improperly maintained air tankers had crashed, including a dramatic 2002 crash, caught on video, where a plane's wings fell off in midair.) Aero Union never did get its planes back into the air, and when the company folded, it could sell them only for spare parts.

Then there was the question of whose job it was to put out the Texas fires. As a federal agency, the Forest Service is responsible for managing fires only on the federal property it oversees. McCaul was pressuring the Forest Service to send out its tankers, but 99.9 percent of the land on fire lay beyond the agency's responsibility. Tom Harbour, the Forest Service's director for fire and aviation management, subtly reminded McCaul that the congressman was pressing for federal help to meet state and local government responsibilities. "We are here," Harbour said, "because our friends in the Texas Forest Service asked us to help. We are pleased to be able to do so."[9] And why was federal help so badly needed? Just as Texans were demanding the feds fly in aerial tankers, the Texas state government was cutting support for its own forest service. Four years later, residents in the same part of Texas inflamed protests against a U.S. Army training exercise, which many local residents around Bastrop suspected was part of a plan to impose martial law. That was simply not true. But the residents noisily opposed the spread of federal power—except when they wanted the federal government to step outside its bounds to help them fight fires that their state government, trimmed back because of budget cuts, could not.

Here was a case in which one of the nation's most vociferous groups of small-government conservatives urgently called on a federal agency to respond, in a way that required the agency to move beyond its authorized responsibility. It responded because it was the right thing to do—mutual aid in times of trouble is good policy, good politics, and effective government. Critics often savage the federal government's power, except when they need it, and when they need it, they want it immediately. Then, when the U.S. Forest Service quickly responded, it did not come to the rescue with assets it owned but with aerial tankers from private contractors working for the feds. We want a small government, except when we need a big government. When government responds, we do not much care which level of government arrives as long as the problem is solved, and much of the problem solving comes through complex partnerships with the private sector.

Representative McCaul's attack on big government while arguing for help for his constituents proved popular. He was reelected in 2014, winning 62 percent of the vote. But there's an irony here: A poll in February 2015 by the University of Texas and the *Texas Tribune* found that just 23 percent of citizens in the Lone Star State had a favorable view of the federal government. Among those surveyed, 57 percent saw the federal government unfavorably, including 36 percent who saw it "very unfavorably." State and local governments did better, with 50 percent favorable for the state government and 46 percent for local government.[10] When the fires threatened, however, McCaul called on the federal government for help. Pressures for quick government response often push the federal government to the foreground of action, even though citizens—and often their elected representatives—say they don't trust the federal government to begin with. No matter how much we dislike government, we're quick to call on it when trouble threatens.

We have come a long way from the Progressives' bipartisan vision of an effective government, with its power constrained by clear boundaries. We have ended up with a bigger government, where the boundaries are anything but clear. All we know is that we want what we want, and we are happy to blind ourselves to the ironic paradoxes scattered along the way. We want a smaller government, except when we want a government that takes care of our problems. We do not like government, but we expect it will perform well when we need it. This pattern works, on one level, because it allows us to have our democratic cake and eat it too. But it increases tension in government. It undermines public trust in government's actions. It muddies our sense of who is in charge of what, and it disconnects citizens from the government they are paying for. When it works, it does not work as well as it should. Because it's so complicated, it sometimes does not work at all. It is a clear case of government failing to adapt to the challenges it faces, and that makes it a symptom of Jurassic government. We clearly need a better strategy to do what we want to have done.

HOW TO DO WHAT MUST BE DONE

As the century-long consensus on competence has eroded, the big question remains: How *will* we do what we must get done? Conservatives and liberals, Republicans and Democrats might well have different answers. A good answer will not magically sweep away political disputes, but without some answer, there is no chance of recovering faith in American democracy. And without even recognizing the importance of the question, there is no hope of getting started. If it does not adapt, America's Jurassic government will be well on the path to extinction.

If we as a nation—and the leaders we elect to govern us—are to escape Madison's warning of wretchedness, we need a new plan for connecting the *what* of government with its *how*. The Progressive tradition served as the foundation of much of what America accomplished in the 20th century. We now need a reboot of that tradition to Progressive 2.0, a commitment to good governance that can transcend partisanship and achieve today what the first phase of Progressivism did for more than a century.

Let me outline six basic truths here—truths that all of us must come to grips with. They must become self-evident and provide the backbone for genuine leadership. I explore these truths more fully in the chapters that follow.

1. Government cannot shrink (much). Conservatives will not let liberals grow it. Demographic trends, especially with a growing population of graying baby boomers, will not let conservatives shrink it. Citizens increasingly expect that government will solve the problems they face, from protecting against terrorism to defending against Ebola. What is inside government's basket of services will surely change, but its overall size will not. In fact, at least as a share of the economy, government has not changed much for 50 years. What is past is prologue.

2. Government does hard things (compared with the private sector) and it is not going to stop. We expect it to provide health care for veterans, ensure food safety, deal with the aftermath of big storms, and fight cybercrime and terrorism. Government does what the private sector will not or cannot do. And when big problems develop, like the shrapnel-filled airbags built by private companies for private carmakers in the early 2010s, a predictable chorus follows: Why didn't government prevent these problems—and what is government going to do about fixing them?

3. Government does much of what it does by interweaving its work with the nongovernmental world, so government's footprint will only increase. Many of the federal government's programs are managed through proxies in the private and nonprofit worlds. Consider Medicare and Medicaid. Together they account for 20 percent of the budget, but they are managed by just 0.2 percent of all federal employees. How does that work? Government does not directly manage the programs—it manages those in private and nonprofit hospitals, clinics, and nursing homes who actually deliver them. The same pattern spills across many of the federal government's activities, including the deceptively complex puzzles at the bottom of fighting the Texas wildfires.

4. *The combination of these truths makes it harder for government to deliver.* It is intrinsically more difficult to do hard things and to do them through proxies. There are good reasons for both. Government's role has expanded to harder things because the public expects government to do more. It has relied on proxy patterns because they allow more flexibility, and they bring expertise into government that it does not have on its own. The strategy has been attractive to many liberals because it has allowed them to expand government's reach without making government bureaucracy bigger. It has been attractive to many conservatives because they have been able to swallow a larger government as long as the private sector delivered it. But these proxies are harder to manage. It is no accident that to improve management of the 32 programs listed as most prone to waste, fraud, and abuse by the federal watchdog agency, the Government Accountability Office, every one of them required smart managers who understood how to build strong horizontal connections among vertical silos. That is a direct product of the drift away from the original Progressive movement's reliance on strong boundaries to get government's work done.

5. *Starving the beast only undermines performance.* Fed up with the growing reach of government, conservatives have tried to cut government (see points 1 and 2). Their odds of winning this battle have not improved (see point 1). If they cannot cut the programs directly, they have been tempted to starve government of the capacity it needs to manage them. That has been the strategy for conservatives opposed

to Obamacare: If they cannot kill it, perhaps they can destroy its ability to work. The starve-the-beast strategy, however, has only worsened public trust in government because it has only reinforced the public's sense that government cannot get its job done. The contentious but important battle over what government should do has been a recurring theme within the Progressive movement for far more than a century. Undermining the *how* of government instead of changing the *what* of its functions, however, has only undermined government's capacity to do its job without fundamentally leading the government to do less of it. That, in turn, has proven dangerous to the performance of public institutions and the public's trust in them.

6. *The failure to perform is bad policy, bad politics, and bad democracy.* Undermining government's ability to deliver, therefore, is not good for anyone. The point in George W. Bush's administration where polling showed his negatives higher than his positives, and from which he never recovered, was the aftermath of Hurricane Katrina, where the government clearly had failed its citizens. Barack Obama fell into a similar trap of distrust after the failed launch of the Obamacare website, when citizens trying to sign up for the program encountered online services that could not deliver. His poll numbers gradually pulled free of the performance-failure flypaper, but only because the administration's political operatives realized they were close to falling into Bush's trap. It is certain that future presidents will have their own versions of the Katrina/Obamacare crisis: huge, and usually unexpected, management problems that undermine performance, diminish trust, and reduce political support. In the short run, that can prove politically fatal; in the long run, that can even further weaken the ability of American government to adapt—and risk sending it down the path that doomed the sauropods, the giants of the Jurassic period whose failure to adapt led them to extinction.

CAN WE AFFORD A GOVERNMENT
THAT DOES NOT WORK?

We can—surely will—and ought to continue to fiercely debate what government ought to do. We can even temporarily trick ourselves into thinking that the execution of government programs does not matter, or that we can fight rearguard actions against programs we do not like by undermining government's ability to execute them. But, like it or not, we built the government we have, we do not show any real sign of rolling it back, and we expect it to deliver on a host of promises it has made. We cannot afford a Jurassic government that fails to adapt.

Consider ten government programs that simply must work.

1. Air-traffic control. The Federal Aviation Administration (FAA) manages the nation's system for steering planes from takeoff to landing. In 2011 air passengers clocked 815 billion revenue passenger miles (one passenger paying to fly one mile). That number is projected to nearly double to 1.57 trillion by 2032.[11] Those passengers expect that the government will get them there safely. Everyone expects that when they arrive at the airport, the system will deliver them safely to their destinations but, in August 2015, a software upgrade glitch at an FAA regional center left hundreds of planes grounded and thousands of passengers fuming.

2. Care for veterans. Millions of Americans have served their country in the armed forces, and many have come back with serious injuries and ongoing illnesses. However, investigative reporters, first in Arizona and then across the nation, discovered in 2014 that too many vets were having to wait far too long to receive medical care. Vets expect that, following their service, they will receive the care that the government promised—and Americans insist that the promises will be kept. The failure of the Department of Veterans Affairs (VA) to deliver rightly stirred outrage among vets, members of Congress, and citizens.

3. Weather satellite data. The National Oceanographic and Atmospheric Administration manages a fleet of weather satellites that provides the key data and photos that help forecasters everywhere predict the weather we will have.[12] Private forecasters rely on these national satellites for the numbers and satellite images they display on their local forecasts, and there are no plans to replace government satellites with private ones. The satellites are vulnerable, and coverage in some places is thin. If a satellite fails, there could be critical gaps as big storms approach the coast. Americans expect the government to warn of approaching weather that could threaten lives and property, even while they are unaware that the government is the source of the weather data on which their favorite private forecasts online and from local media are dependent.

4. Improper payments. In 2014 the federal government made $125 billion in improper payments. Two-thirds of the problem came from just three programs—the Medicare and Medicaid programs in the Department of Health and Human Services and the Earned Income program in the Department of the Treasury.[13] Taxpayers expect that their hard-earned dollars will not go to waste.

5. Cybersecurity. Cyberthreats have grown from a few rogue attacks to a genuine national and economic security issue. In 2014 the North Korean government's assault on Sony Pictures transformed its effort to stop the release of a movie about a fictional attempt to assassinate the country's leader into an international political and business crisis. At the VA, where the troubled department was struggling to transform itself by relying more on telemedicine and sophisticated electronic records systems, there were more than a billion cyberattacks in March 2015 alone.[14] Intrusions into both private and governmental systems have become an enormous security risk. Americans expect that they will be kept safe from cyberattacks and that the government services on which they depend will not be destroyed by a computer collapse.

6. Bridge safety. There are 610,749 bridges in the country, and the Federal Highway Administration determined in 2014 that 61,365— 10 percent—were structurally deficient.[15] In 2007 a structurally deficient bridge on I-35W in Minneapolis collapsed and 13 people died. Americans expect that government will prevent bridges from collapsing as they are driving across them.

7. Airport screening. The U.S. Transportation Security Administration processes 1.8 million travelers every day through its airport checkpoints, to ensure that no one is bringing anything dangerous on board airplanes. Citizens expect that they will be able to fly safely without fear of a terrorist attack.

8. Safe drinking water. In January 2014 residents in West Virginia turned on their taps one morning and found the water smelled strongly of black licorice. Some residents went to local hospitals with nausea and eye infections. Some of the hospitals decided to limit surgeries. As we will explore in more detail in chapter 5, a tank in a chemical plant had sprung a leak and spilled toxins into the local water supply. Citizens expect that government will ensure that their drinking water will not make them sick.

9. Investor protection, part 1. In the years leading up to the 2008 financial crisis, many banks issued mortgages for more than properties were worth, packaged them together in financial instruments that almost no one understood, sold them to investors who believed they were getting a good deal, and then proved unable to halt the collapse when housing prices fell and the mortgage investments proved shoddy. Citizens expect that the government will protect them from misrepresentation and other shady practices by investment companies.

10. Investor protection, part 2. In 2010 the stock market's Dow Jones average mysteriously dropped more than 1,000 points in just a few seconds. As they investigated, government officials determined that a single trader had used sophisticated computer programs and high-speed trading to plunge the market into crisis. In an instant, he wiped out a trillion dollars' worth of equity. Fortunately, the market quickly recovered. But investors expected that the government would ensure stability in the financial markets on which the economy depends.

These issues are important, complex, and increasingly international. Consider an eleventh example: the challenge of keeping our food chain safe. More than 90 percent of the seafood we eat in the United States is produced abroad, half in fish farms. An excursion to a local supermarket makes the point that it is much more than seafood that is globalized. On a recent trip, I found snails from Indonesia, smoked oysters from China, crispy onions and canned mushrooms from the Netherlands, anchovies from Morocco, and artichoke hearts from Peru. There were veggies that simply said "packed in the USA," but the label did not say where they had been grown. Our food chain is increasingly long, ever more global, and out of the government's direct control. But even though the job is hard, we still expect the government to make sure every bite of our food is healthy, every time.

This is what we expect government to do, but the institution is unquestionably struggling to do it. Our expectations are growing, government's performance is falling short, and it is becoming increasingly clear that we need a fresh approach to government to do what we expect it to do. The Progressives' foundation worked remarkably well until it ran out of gas. What we need now is a reinvented strategy, based on a renewed bipartisan commitment to making government work, holding it accountable, and matching its capacity to the challenges of the 21st century. We need, in short, a reboot, with a Progressive 2.0 to align government's capacity with the jobs we expect it to do.

What would this look like? We fight most over the issues that, in fact, are most settled: what government ought to do. We ignore the issues that are most in play and whose consequences are critical to government in the 21st century: how government can best do what it sets out to do. A renewed commitment to competence must crack this dual dilemma of focusing attention on the right questions and developing far-reaching answers that help government deliver.

In the chapters that follow, I explore how we can do so. The answers are based in three building blocks. The first is *people*: getting the right people with the right skills in the right places at the right time. Government—along with society in general—is becoming more complex, more interconnected, and more international, yet too often more caught in deep silos with thick walls. The biggest problems plaguing American government require bridging the boundaries between organizations that share responsibility for delivering results. The greater the complexity, the more we must rely on individual leaders with strong bridge-building instincts. The original Progressive tradition built the foundation. It began with the passage of the Civil Service Reform Act in 1883, an act sponsored by a Democrat (George Pendleton from Ohio), drafted by a reformer (Dorman Bridgeman Eaton from Vermont), and signed by a Republican (Chester A. Arthur from New York). They reflected a nonpartisan commitment to a professional government. The commitment to competence needs to demonstrate that a professional government with the capacity to get the job done serves even the most fiercely partisan players. The harder the things that government tries to do, the more important that professionalism becomes—and government is not about to give up on doing hard things.

The second building block is greater skill in managing the *interweaving of government*. Government is less and less a solitary actor and far more a partner—with other government agencies, other levels of government, other sectors (including the private and nonprofit), and other governments—in getting its work done. Over the course of the 20th century, government has gradually woven an ever-more-complex fabric of action, one different from the threads used to create the modern American state. If government is to be effective, it needs tools that cope with this vast increase in interwoven action.

The third building block is *evidence and information*. An information age government, quite simply, needs evidence and technology to guide it. Evidence provides feedback on what works. Technology vastly enhances efficiency. It crosses the boundaries that bureaucratic structures cannot. And technology creates opportunities to link citizens with their government. As the delivery of government services gets more and more complex, with government relying on a vast network of interconnected proxies, many of which are outside government, technology can provide a laser-like link for accountability. The original Progressive movement empowered government and held it accountable through structures and processes, carefully constrained. Since government has evolved into a system where structures and processes are no longer the basic building blocks, with the tools and mission falling out of sync in a Jurassic government, we need a replacement. In Progressive 2.0, that is evidence and technology.

I spell out the case for a new government, with a fresh commitment to competence, in the pages that follow. In a remarkably bipartisan way, Republicans and Democrats alike relied for generations on Progressivism, often for different partisan goals. But that tradition failed to adapt as government's challenges grew and no longer delivers the goods and services that citizens and policymakers expect. And it certainly no longer advances a government that citizens can trust and in which they have faith.

It is scarcely surprising that American politics today is nasty. The nation's governance has always been a full-contact sport. It surely was when the founders met in Philadelphia to write the Declaration of Independence and then to draft the Constitution, and it always will be. But today's political atmosphere is also a reflection of the profound uneasiness, often unspoken, about government's ability to deliver results as well as its deep intrusion into our lives. Progressive 1.0 was built to solve delivery of government services. But the model is outdated, and that is why we need the renewed commitment to competence.

This time, however, the stakes are even higher. As the 2008 financial collapse demonstrated, and as the 2014 Ebola outbreak underlined, a problem anywhere can quickly become a problem everywhere. The 24-hour news cycle shines a harsh spotlight on problems and gives government officials little time to react before political judgments crystallize. The founders of the nation anticipated a more leisurely process to find consensus in political disputes. The challenges of the 21st century do not allow the leisure that the system demands. But the founders also anticipated that government would work well on behalf of the country's citizens, and they expected that subsequent generations would figure out how to make that happen. That is the challenge of our age, and it is the great question for which Progressive 2.0 is the answer.

We can and will—and should—continue to fight fiercely over what government should do. We might even fight about issues that are long settled. But as we fight over the *what* of policy, we ignore the usually neglected questions about the *how* at our peril. It is bad politics not to deliver on promises, no matter which party makes them. And if citizens lose confidence in government's ability to deliver on its word, it is even worse for citizens' trust in their government. We should not pretend we can erase partisanship. That would be folly, since it cannot be done, and it would not be smart, since lively, even raucous, debate is healthy for a democracy's soul. What we do need is a new consensus that whatever we decide as a country to do, we have an obligation to citizens to do well. We need to reclaim our government by recovering the lost commitment to competence. In the pages that follow, I explore how. If we fail to adapt, we will slip ever deeper into Jurassic government, and we know from the dinosaurs how that will turn out.

TWO

Government's Size
Can't Change (Much)

W<small>E HAVE LONG DEBATED HOW</small> big government ought to be. However, perhaps to the surprise of most citizens, the growth of governmental power has been remarkably bipartisan. Truman created the Department of Defense and Eisenhower the Department of Health, Education, and Welfare (that is a Democrat reorganizing national defense and a Republican strengthening welfare). Johnson added two new departments for Transportation and for Housing and Urban Development. Nixon wanted to cut the number of departments down to just eight, with State, Justice, Treasury, and Defense at the core, with the remaining departments reorganized into Economic Affairs, Natural Resources, Human Resources, and Community Development. His plan failed, but he did knock the Post Office out of the cabinet. Carter created new departments for Education and Energy. Reagan elevated the Veterans Administration to cabinet status. George W. Bush created the Department of Homeland Security. Since World

War II, Democrats have advanced four new departments and split one (Department of Health, Education, and Welfare) into two (Department of Health and Human Services and Department of Education); Republicans have created three new departments and demoted one.

Government's role is huge, and it is even bigger than we realize. It is impossible to get out of bed in the morning without encountering government; it is very likely most of us do not recognize the encounter. With luck, there would have been a good night's sleep, on a mattress and pillows that carried government labels (along with the famous warning that removing the label is a violation of federal law— although it is perfectly legal for a consumer to do so). The sleep might (actually, should) have been protected by smoke alarms and sprinklers. An electric alarm clock would have been powered by wiring dictated by local building codes to make sure that the walls do not ignite—and, for that matter, local building codes also ensure that the walls and floors do not collapse. If the sleeper were gently awakened with favorite tunes on a smartphone, there would have been protection from both American but also European governmental regulations. (The *CE* marking on the back of many electronic devices stands for "Conformité Européenne," certifying that the device met the standards for the European Economic Area.) In fact, a careful reading of the inside of a smartphone or of the inserts in the packaging is a grand tour through transnational governmental regulation.

Splashing water on the face to wake up requires encountering the local government's water system, operated under federal water quality standards. The Energy Policy Act of 1992 set a maximum flow for the toilet at 1.6 gallons per flush. Toothpaste labeling is set by federal regulation. The same is true for cosmetics, including skin moisturizers, deodorants, makeup, and fingernail polish. In the United States and around the world, the lightbulbs helping the sleeper find footing have been regulated to reduce the amount of energy they use. And all of this is even before the sleeper thinks about breakfast—along with the labeling requirements on the cereal, the regulations on milk, and safety oversight on the toaster and stove. There are separate rules for the refrigerator, including what coolant it uses and what energy labeling standards it must meet. If our groggy sleeper switches on the television to catch up on the news and weather, more regulations kick in to govern the safety of the TV's wiring and radiation emissions, the cost of the cable service bringing the signal to the set, and the licensing of the station broadcasting the show. When stepping into the shower, our now-awake sleeper confronts government regulations concerning showerheads, shampoo, and shower doors (but not soap, unless the soap is used to treat a skin condition, such as acne). And that is before reaching for a towel, laundered in a washing machine and dryer built with extensive government standards for energy efficiency, with the help of laundry detergent subject to its own rules on safety and the use of phosphorous, to prevent local waterways from turning green with algae-based slime.

Government is even bigger than we think, with a deeper reach into our lives than we realize. Every rule is an effort to solve a problem that the government decided required a public solution. Those rules are unlikely to be rolled back, not only because that process would be hard but also because the underlying problems remain problems and continue to demand solutions. Understanding why requires an excursion through government, how it compares, and what forces are shaping it.

AMERICAN GOVERNMENT IS LARGE IN SIZE—BUT MIDDLING COMPARED WITH THE REST OF THE WORLD

Although this certainly does not fit popular perceptions, the size of government in the United States, compared with the rest of the industrialized world, is decidedly average. Consider the 32 nations in the Organization for Economic Cooperation and Development (OECD), the collection of the world's advanced economies. The United States has fewer government employees as a share of the workforce (14.4 percent in 2011, compared with the OECD average of 15.4 percent).[1]

Americans might feel sometimes that they are overrun by bureaucrats, especially federal bureaucrats. But just one in eight government bureaucrats work for the federal government, and just one in eight federal bureaucrats work in the Washington metropolitan area. Compared with the rest of the world, government bureaucracy in the United States is pretty typical—except that, because of its system of federalism, it has a smaller concentration of its government workers in the capital.[2]

What about government spending? Here again, the United States is typical. Government, at all levels, spends a bit less than OECD nations as a share of the economy—41.7 percent (in 2011) for the United States, versus 45.4 percent for the OECD as a whole.[3] Spending per citizen is 23 percent higher in the United States than the OECD average, but that is due in part to higher defense spending. Even so, it is about the same on a per capita basis as France and Belgium.[4] Compared with the world's major democracies, what most stands out is how average American government spending is, how much of government's work happens at the state and local level, and how fortunate Americans are to have such wealth to support their governments.

Thus, America is not overrun by government bureaucrats, in comparison with the rest of the world. At the federal and state levels, government employment has been flat since the beginning of the Reagan years. Local government employment has risen, but that is because local governments have hired more teachers, police officers, firefighters, and sanitation workers to serve a growing population (see figure 2-1).

CUTTING THE SIZE OF GOVERNMENT IS HARD

Slowing the pace of government spending turns out to be very hard to do, not only in the United States but around the world. No one tried harder than British Prime Minister Margaret Thatcher, who launched an aggressive budget-cutting program in the 1980s. She privatized government-owned British Airways, as well as ports, an

Figure 2-1. Government Employment

Employment in thousands of workers

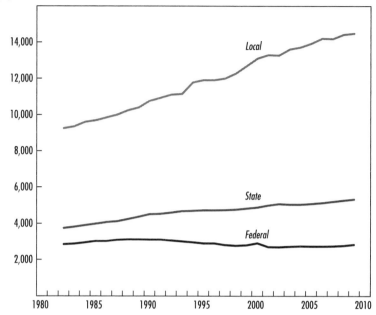

Source: U.S. Census Bureau, Governments Division, "Federal, State, and Local Govern-ments, Public Employment and Payroll Data," May 2011 (www.census.gov/compendia/statab/2012/tables/12s0461.xls).

oil company, a steel producer, the telephone company, and water and gas utilities. She sold high-prestige state-owned brands, including Jaguar and Rolls-Royce. In the United States, Ronald Reagan likewise tried to cut government. He did not have the same portfolio of state-owned companies to sell, but he did launch a major privatization initiative, which meant contracting out more government services to private companies. Because of the steps he took, it is difficult to find a government security officer guarding most government buildings, a government cafeteria worker providing food in government lunchrooms, or a government custodian cleaning government offices. Thatcher and Reagan stood together as allies in the government-cutting movement, and leaders around the world tried to follow their lead.

Figure 2-2. Government Spending in the United Kingdom and the United States
Percent of GDP

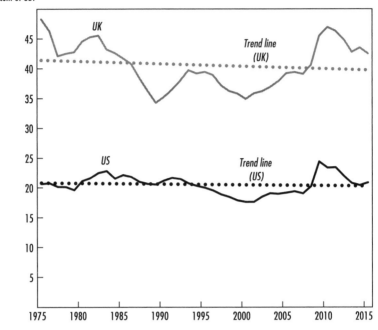

Source: Congressional Budget Office and Her Majesty's Treasury.

But how much did they actually change the long-term direction of government spending? The results are surprisingly modest, as figure 2-2 shows. Both managed to bend down the long-term spending curve— but only by a little. In both the United Kingdom and the United States, government spending in 2015 was about the same as what it was 35 years before.

TOTAL FEDERAL SPENDING HASN'T CHANGED MUCH—BUT THE INSIDE OF THE BUDGET HAS

There is a common perception that federal spending has exploded in recent decades. Of course, spending is up—but so too is the cost of living. What if we look at federal spending after controlling for infla-

Figure 2-3. Federal Spending as a Percentage of GDP

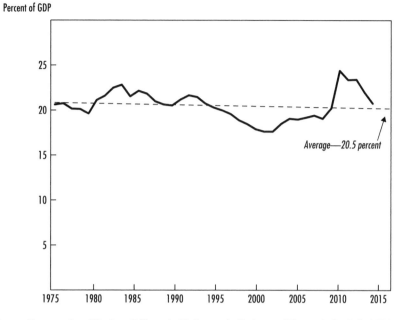

Percent of GDP

Source: Congressional Budget Office, *An Update to the Budget and Economic Outlook: 2014 to 2024* (Washington, D.C., August 2014), table 3 (www.cbo.gov/publication/45653).

tion? In fact, since 1970, government spending as a share of the economy (the gross domestic product, the total amount of goods and services produced in the country) has been relatively steady. There have been some bounces because of big economic swings, most notably the 2008 economic collapse (as the economy shrank and short-term federal spending to boost the economy grew). Overall, however, federal spending averaged 20.5 percent of the gross domestic product from 1974 through 2013 (see figure 2-3), on an ever so slightly downward curve. If we look at federal spending and federal government employment, however, a different story emerges. There isn't an ever-growing number of federal bureaucrats. Federal employment has been flat while federal spending per bureaucrat has soared. That is a different picture from at the state and local level, where spending has been flatter (see figure 2-4).

Figure 2-4. Government Spending per Bureaucrat

Millions of dollars of spending per 1,000 employees

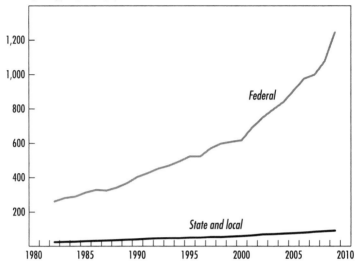

Sources: U.S. Office of Management and Budget, *Budget of the United States Government: Fiscal Year 2015—Historical Tables* (2014), table 15-2; and U.S. Census Bureau, Governments Division, "Federal, State, and Local Governments—Public Employment and Payroll Data," May 2011.

How could this be? After controlling for inflation, federal spending has not gone up. But what the federal government spends its budget on has changed—a lot. As figure 2-5 shows, spending for mandatory programs has more than doubled, from 5.6 percent of GDP (in 1965) to 13.8 percent (in 2014). Spending for discretionary programs, on the other hand, has fallen almost in half, from 10.9 percent to 6.8 percent. State and local spending, in contrast, goes mainly for functions that depend on the population: police, fire, sanitation, and highways.

There are even more dramatic changes inside these numbers. From 1974 to 2013, discretionary spending shrank, especially in defense, which is down more than 30 percent after allowing for inflation (see table 2-1). Social Security and income security (welfare programs)

Figure 2-5. Changes inside the Federal Budget

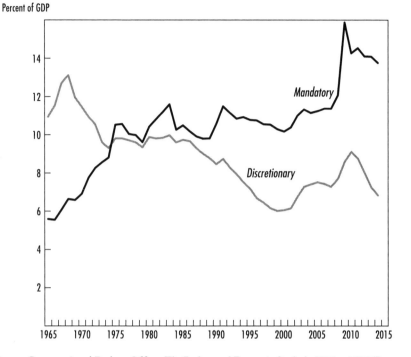

Percent of GDP

Source: Congressional Budget Office, *The Budget and Economic Outlook: 2015 to 2025* (January 2015), table 3 (www.cbo.gov/publication/45069).

Table 2-1. Changes in the Composition of Federal Spending

OUTLAYS AS PERCENTAGE OF GDP	1974	2013	CHANGE
Defense	5.4	3.8	−30.7%
Nondefense	3.9	3.5	−10.4%
Social Security	3.7	4.9	31.3%
Medicare	0.7	3.5	389.4%
Medicaid	0.4	1.6	308.2%
Income security	1.2	2.0	66.7%
All other	1.4	0.2	−85.7%

Source: Congressional Budget Office, Office of Management and Budget.

are up. Spending for health care programs (principally Medicare and Medicaid) vastly expanded. The story of "big government," at least on the budget side, is the story of growing entitlements and the shrinking of almost everything else—even as total government spending remained relatively flat. We are not overrun by federal bureaucrats. We are simply spending much more on the promises we made in the 1960s to cover more of the costs of health care, especially for the elderly. And we have done it without increasing the number of bureaucrats.

THE SIZE OF THE FEDERAL GOVERNMENT IN THE FUTURE WILL BE SHAPED BY FORCES ALREADY IN MOTION

In 2011 *Washington Post* columnist Ezra Klein quipped that the federal government is "an insurance conglomerate protected by a large, standing army."[5] He got that just about right. The need for a strong national defense surely will not diminish. Defense spending in the early years of the 2010s was actually below the level of the post-Vietnam generation, when measured as a share of the economy, and it is unlikely to shrink much.[6] Meanwhile, spending for programs for older Americans will surely grow. The elderly for the next two generations have already been born, their numbers are increasing, and government is unlikely to walk away from its commitments, especially in health care. In 2015 Americans over the age of 65 accounted for about 15 percent of the population (see table 2-2). By 2030 the share will grow by more than a third, to 20.6 percent. Even more dramatic is the coming growth in what demographers call the "oldest old." Americans over the age of 85 were 2 percent of the population in 2015. By 2045 the share will more than double to 4.4 percent. Baby Boomers will unquestionably drive federal spending up as they retire and age, but Millennials will be an even bigger engine of government

Table 2-2. The Graying of America

Percent of total
population

AGE	2015	2030	2045	2060
Under 18 years	22.9	21.2	20.3	19.7
18 to 24 years	9.7	8.6	8.3	8.0
25 to 44 years	26.3	26.7	25.2	24.7
45 to 64 years	26.1	22.9	24.5	24.0
65 years and over	14.9	20.6	21.8	23.6
85 years and over	2.0	2.5	4.4	4.7

Source: U.S. Bureau of the Census, *2014 National Population Projections* (2014) (www.census
.gov/population/projections/data/national/2014/summarytables.html).

spending. By 2060 their "oldest old" will account for almost 5 percent of the nation's population. By 2030 federal spending for senior citizens will account for half of the federal budget (see figure 2-6), and there is no sign that number will—or can—drop. By 2084 some analysts expect, 60 percent of the federal budget will go to the elderly, if present trends continue.

Liberals might want to increase government spending, but there is not going to be much new money to spend. Economic forecasters expect that the coming decade will see only modest economic growth, so increases in revenue will follow suit. The Congressional Budget Office expects growth of about 2.2 percent a year through 2025, slower than in the 1980s and 1990s because the labor force will not expand much.[7] That will not generate enough tax money to cover the costs of retiring Baby Boomers, let alone new government programs. The federal debt will continue to hang over the economy, stuck between 75 and 80 percent of the gross domestic product.[8] There simply will not be new money to fund many new programs.

Figure 2-6. Spending Surge for Seniors

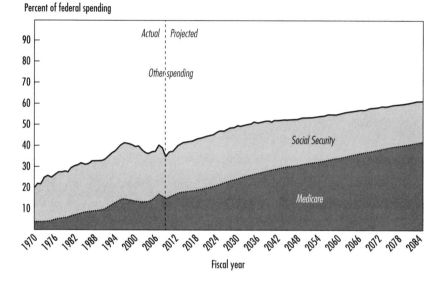

Percent of federal spending

Fiscal year

Source: Veronique de Rugy, "Spending Surge for Seniors: Medicare and Social Security Total 50 Percent of Budget by 2030" (Arlington, Va.: Mercatus Center, George Mason University, December 19, 2011) (http://mercatus.org/publication/spending-surge-seniors -medicare-and-social-security-total-50-percent-budget-2030).

On the other hand, although conservatives might want to cut government spending, most of the federal government's budget is locked up in entitlements, defense, and interest on the debt. In 2014 these categories accounted for 91 percent of the federal budget—with the remaining 9 percent taken up by the cost of everything else the federal government does. There is little support for cutting these discretionary programs, and even big cuts would not considerably reduce overall federal spending. These debates are philosophically important, and they are sure to produce a great deal of heat. It is impossible to imagine any conceivable collection of cuts in discretionary spending that would produce a cut in federal spending that would really matter.

So, for better or worse, the size of the federal government—how much we spend, and how many people we employ to manage federal programs—is mostly stuck. It is possible to reduce federal employment by contracting out more programs and shifting other programs into quasi-public corporations. Reformers, for example, have proposed transferring air-traffic controllers into a private or quasi-public corporation. That would change the labels on the door and the body count of federal employees. But it would not fundamentally change the government's size or its impact on our lives. It would, however, surely make the system more complicated to govern.

STATE AND LOCAL GOVERNMENT SPENDING HAS LEVELED OFF AND WILL LIKELY STAY THERE

At the state and local level, spending has plateaued as well. There was a spurt in spending from 1971 through 2000, even after controlling for inflation and population growth, of 78 percent. Since the mid-2000s, however, spending has stabilized.

Table 2-3 tells the tale. From 1971 through 2011, state and local spending grew by 78 percent, with the biggest burst in the 1980s. Since

Table 2-3. Change in State and Local Spending

Percent change

YEARS	EDUCATION	HIGHWAYS	WELFARE	OTHER	TOTAL
1971–2011	50	−12	183	104	78
1971–1980	4	−15	20	31	13
1981–1990	23	10	28	35	28
1991–2000	16	7	25	10	14
2001–2011	−3	−9	21	−1	1

Source: Calculated from Council of Economic Advisers, *Economic Report of the President: 2014* (Washington, D.C., 2014), table B-24 (http://goo.gl/UXvGE5; http://goo.gl/8PSWMv).

Figure 2-7. Change in State and Local Government Spending

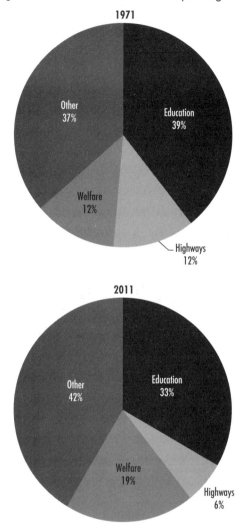

Source: Council of Economic Advisers, *Economic Report of the President, 2014* (Washington, D.C.: 2014) (http://goo.gl/dJuwPT).

2011, in part because of anti-spending pressures from groups such as the Tea Party movement and in part because of slow growth in revenues, spending leveled off. Traditional state and local programs, such as those benefiting education and highways, along with general programs like police, fire, and sanitation departments, have stabilized or declined. The big spending increases have come in welfare, including Medicaid, where states split the cost with the federal government. Snapshots of state and local budgets 40 years apart, in 1971 and 2011, show a different picture (see figure 2-7), as welfare programs (including health care) have gradually gobbled up revenue, just as they have at the federal level.

State and local governments have struggled to balance their spending for these health care costs with the demand for traditional programs, from schools to police and fire protection. In fact, the U.S. Government Accountability Office forecast that state and local governments could face structural deficits for the next fifty years. The biggest driver of the forecast was predictable: the rising costs of Medicaid and the expense for health care benefits for government employees and retirees, which increasingly are crowding out spending for other programs.[9]

State and local fiscal pressures are slightly different from at the federal level because of their revenue structures and the large number of basic services that state and local governments provide on the front lines. But there are two important similarities. First, the aging population will keep up the pressure on state and local spending, just as it will at the federal level. Second, these trends make it impossible to reduce overall spending significantly, while public opposition to higher taxes makes it unlikely that spending will grow. That is why state and local government spending leveled off in the 2000s, and this uneasy equilibrium is likely to continue far into the future.

THE SIZE IS STUCK

Since the early 1990s there have been wild and raucous debates over the size of government. Conservatives have loudly called for shrinking the government's appetite for tax dollars; liberals have more quietly but just as firmly pushed back. The nation battled the second-worst economic downturn since the Depression. It emerged with one of the longest recoveries on record, even if it also proved one of the most rugged and uneven. These political and economic tugs have, perhaps surprisingly, produced an equilibrium—a rickety, troubled, and unstable one, but an equilibrium in government's size nonetheless. One could imagine epic forces that could upset this balance: a major international crisis, which could require World War II levels of spending; a sustained economic collapse, which could require massive governmental intervention; accelerating climate change, which could nudge a reluctant nation toward expensive adaptation; or a completely unexpected crisis, which could bring a fundamental reset to government's size and function. But absent the unexpected, the size of government is likely to be stuck and to stay stuck for a long time.

There will, of course, be truly fierce battles at the margin. Neither conservatives nor liberals are likely to win the fight over the size of government. They are far more likely to descend into trench warfare over small pieces of government turf. That was what happened when battlefield gridlock emerged in World War I, and it is likely to be the near- to medium-term future of debates about government in the United States.

Compounding the dilemma is the relative ignorance of most Americans about just how they spend their tax dollars. In 2015 the Kaiser Family Foundation released a poll on how much Americans thought the nation was spending on foreign aid. Responses ranged as high as half of the budget or more, for 10 percent of the respondents. The average guess: 26 percent. The actual amount: less than 1 percent.

More than half of those surveyed said they thought the country was spending too much on foreign aid. When asked whether they thought 1 percent was too much, 60 percent said that amount would be "too little" or "about the right amount."[10] A 2010 survey, in fact, suggested that 10 percent of the budget should go to foreign aid.[11] So not only is there no agreement on what to cut, there is little understanding about where the money goes to begin with. There is shaky consensus on how money is actually being spent. And there's no consensus on spending it differently.

Details about what government does are complicated, and they are often buried in hard-to-decipher documents. The media tend to cover the horse race aspects of policy far more than the details of what the races are about, and our policy debates drift far from substance into ideology. Some international surveys, moreover, rank the knowledge of American voters as middling at best. Sustainable Government Indicators, a European-based research think tank, studied the degree to which citizens are knowledgeable about policy issues. They found in 2014, in the United States, "few citizens are well-informed of government policies; most citizens have only a rudimental knowledge of policies," which put Americans in the same group with France, Greece, Lithuania, and Mexico, among others—and far behind Finland, Iceland, Sweden, Norway, and Denmark.[12] Our citizens lag substantially behind the world's leading democracies in their knowledge of the democracy in which they live.[13]

All of this makes it hard for us to have an honest conversation with ourselves about who we are as a nation and where we want to go. It is easier to fight on matters of high principle if the battles are not constrained by the facts. But, for better or worse, the basic facts about the size of government are not likely to change, and they will not provide us with many choices. Tight budgets and the antigovernment mood put a lid on how much government can grow. Government health care costs for aging Baby Boomers—and the generations behind them—put a limit on how much government can shrink. We will need to make peace with the size of government we have, because it is going to prove mighty hard to change it.

That is why most debates about government are topsy-turvy. The policies already in place, coupled with the nation's demographic trends and its economic pressures, make it difficult to dial spending down (because health care costs for an aging population will be hard to shrink) or dial spending up (because there will be little revenue to pay for it without an unacceptable increase in taxes). We will fight mightily over the size-of-government question, and even the marginal battles can prove epic. The roughest domestic fight of the early 2010s, Obama's Affordable Care Act, did not propose dramatically increasing the nation's spending on health care or changing who provided it. It was about requiring everyone to have insurance and determining how best to subsidize it. It is a huge and important battle. But the program is not likely to create new bureaucracies or vastly change the level of governmental spending.

That leads to an important conclusion: What matters most is not so much the *what* but the *how* of government—how government exercises its role and, increasingly, how it relies on nongovernmental partners to do its work. We turn next to the story of how we got onto this road to begin with.

THREE

People

IN THE SUMMER OF 2008, television news reports were full of stories about an attack of killer tomatoes.[1] First in New Mexico and then in 43 states and the District of Columbia, hundreds of Americans became sick with severe stomach distress. Public health workers frantically struggled to track down the problem. It turned out to be salmonella—but what was its source? Investigators had no proven way of tracking the underlying cause except by painstakingly interviewing victims, asking them what they had eaten, and searching for some common element in their diets. Because salmonella can take several days to develop and it can grow from food purchased long ago, it is tough work. Try to remember what you have eaten at every meal in the past week—and then try to remember when and where you have purchased the food in your refrigerator. The first hints from the investigation suggested that the outbreak might have come from tainted tomatoes, and that led supermarkets around the country to pull tomatoes from their shelves. Newscasters showed California farmers plowing endless acres of tomatoes into the ground because they could not sell them, and many Americans celebrated the Fourth of July without sliced tomatoes on their hamburgers.

But despite these aggressive steps, the disease continued to spread. Tomato growers' financial losses passed $100 million, supermarkets lost business, and consumers panicked. Investigators were befuddled. Just what was the source of the salmonella outbreak? What followed was truly extraordinary sleuthing. Public health workers wondered: If tomatoes were somehow implicated, what restaurants relied on tomatoes? The conclusion: Mexican and Italian restaurants. The investigators then began checking on where the salmonella victims had eaten. They found a link to Mexican restaurants, including victims who ate pico de gallo, corn tortillas, and freshly prepared salsa, but not to Italian eateries. But what was the source of the problem?

To crack the puzzle, public health sleuths turned to a remarkable innovative tool: credit card receipts. There were clusters of cases among those who had eaten at Mexican restaurants, but restaurant patrons could not remember everything they had eaten. It was even harder for investigators to separate out the ingredients in all the dishes and where they had come from. But public health workers were able to use the itemized bills that came with credit cards for some imaginative sleuthing. They first identified the victims and then used the bills to identify which menu items they had eaten. Next they sorted out the dishes that the victims had in common and checked for shared ingredients.

The technique helped Minnesota Department of Health officials probe a cluster of 19 cases that popped up among people who had eaten at a natural food restaurant, who had eaten dishes containing salsa, guacamole, red bell peppers, cilantro, and jalapeño peppers. A week later, a team of public health experts from the North Carolina Division of Public Health, the Mecklenburg County Health Department in Charlotte, and the Centers for Disease Control (CDC) worked on another cluster, this time at a Mexican restaurant. Here they found a single common menu item: guacamole. They checked with the restaurant's chefs and broke the ingredients down: avocado, raw Roma tomatoes, raw red onions, raw Serrano peppers, cilantro, salt, and lime juice. There were some links to the Minnesota cluster. Which ingredient, they wondered, was the culprit?

More sleuthing in the far west led a multiagency investigative team from the Arizona and New Mexico state governments, the Navajo Nation, the Indian Health Service, and the CDC to an important clue. These victims had not eaten at a restaurant—but they had eaten jalapeño peppers and perhaps Serrano peppers. That work, coupled with the credit card analysis, helped investigators narrow their search. Skillful forensic work tracked the national contamination back to a single jalapeño pepper at a food-processing plant in McAllen, Texas—just one pepper from one processing plant, among the millions of possible contaminants. It was a needle-in-a-haystack moment of discovery in exploring an outbreak that sickened 1,442 persons. From the McAllen processing plant, they identified the source: peppers grown at a farm in Tamaulipas, Mexico, which had been irrigated with contaminated water. It was an inspired use of big-data technology to map the complicated food chain—and it brought federal, state, and local public health investigators into a remarkable partnership with restaurateurs, supermarket operators, and farmers.

The case is a microcosm for the enormous food-safety issues facing consumers in America and around the world. The CDC estimates that one in six Americans get sick every year from food-borne illness; 128,000 are hospitalized and 3,000 die.[2] The FDA has the lead in food inspection, but fifteen different federal agencies have a piece of the food-safety responsibilities. As a former FDA food-safety official explained, "There's a lack of understanding where the risks lie. We don't know what we don't know."[3] But what we do know is that the "FDA is not keeping pace with the targets for foreign food inspections set by Congress," as GAO concluded.[4] The government side involves multiple agencies and all levels of government. The private sector side is huge, complex, and global. The food chain is so long and complicated that full inspections are impossible. So, as the 2008 salmonella outbreak demonstrates, the key to food safety is smart government workers armed with good technology and even better instincts.

Food safety is a critically important problem. Keeping consumers from getting sick is essential. So too is preventing massive economic losses for companies that grow, process, and distribute food in the multibillion-dollar industry. Everyone—liberals and conservatives, Democrats and Republicans—agrees that keeping food safe is a goal that government must pursue. Doing so requires the smartest of government strategies, including boundary-spanning technology that bridges the critical pressure points in the system. Making this work requires skilled people—government bureaucrats with the right instincts, the right skills, in the right place at the right time—to do what has to be done. Even if we do not like government, we certainly do insist that government protect our food supply, and that requires smart bureaucrats as the cornerstone of competence. Escaping Jurassic government requires ensuring that bureaucrats keep up with the challenges citizens count on them to solve.

DECLINING INVESTMENT IN PEOPLE

As the demand for competence in government rose in the post–World War II years, however, American government struggled with a growing dilemma: a rising appetite for government programs and a declining appetite for hiring bureaucrats to manage them. Since the 1980s, there have been recurring presidential strategies to cut the number of federal employees. However, despite highly publicized efforts, the overall result has been virtually no change. Ronald Reagan set out to privatize as much of government as he could and to turn its work over to the private sector. But during his administration, federal civilian employment actually *increased* 4 percent, because the administration

Figure 3-1. Federal Executive Branch Employment

Employment in thousands of workers

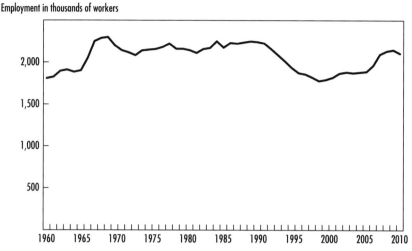

Source: U.S. Office of Personnel Management, "Historical Federal Workforce Tables" (http://goo.gl/uZVDUA).

increased defense spending and it needed federal bureaucrats to manage defense contracts. The Clinton administration took another run at cutting the workforce, through its "reinventing government" movement, and shrank federal employment by 351,000 workers in its first five years.[5] During the George W. Bush administration, federal employment crept back up, especially because the government federalized airport screeners. There was wrenching debate about the size of government in the last third of the 20th century, but the basic story, at least in terms of federal employment, is one of stability. Total federal executive branch employment in 2012 was about the same as it was in 1972: 2.1 million workers (see figure 3-1).

However, Reagan did accelerate a subtle but important change in the nature of government jobs. His privatization campaign shifted a large number of blue-collar government jobs to private companies. This trend was under way long before he took office, and it continued after he left. But he sped up the privatization trend. The result was not so much a decline in the *number* of federal employees but a change in the *composition* of the workforce.

Since the mid-1970s there has been a steady upward creep in the skill level, and the related pay, of federal employees. As figure 3-2 shows, the average level of workers in the General Schedule (GS), the federal government's basic personnel system, has increased constantly, from 6.7 in 1960 to 10.3 in 2014. Policy decisions along the way account for some of this grade creep. For example, some groups of higher-skilled federal employees have been moved in and out of the overall GS over the years. But the changing makeup of the federal workforce is the real story. From 1973 to 2014, the number of administrative employees more than doubled. The number of professional employees increased by 78 percent. Both changes are the product of a more complex collection of federal programs, requiring higher levels of skills—and more contract managers to administer them (see figure 3-3). Clerical positions have declined by 78 percent, which naturally flowed from big changes in workplace technology. And the federal government has become overwhelmingly white collar—91 percent (in 2012), compared with 39 percent in the private sector.[6]

That is the product of more contracting out, since the federal government scarcely has fewer floors and restrooms to clean, fewer vehicles to maintain, or fewer employees who eat lunch. Some of the contracting out is surprising. In the 1980s, I visited the Department of Energy's Rocky Flats plant, not far from Denver. Closed in 1992, the plant was once a high-precision machine shop, manufacturing the "pits," or the cores, for nuclear weapons. The pits were made of plutonium, some of the most dangerous material on the planet, and were always high on the list of the nation's most sensitive secrets. Rocky Flats had multiple layers of security. Visitors were not permitted to go anywhere—even the bathroom—without an escort, and an extra layer of tall fencing topped with razor wire protected the shops. Security often seemed tighter than it was at the White House. And

Figure 3-2. Average GS Level of Federal Employees

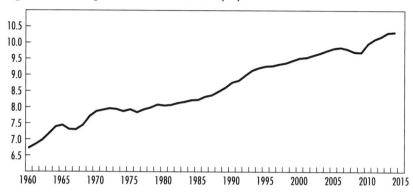

Source: U.S. Office of Personnel Management, Central Personnel Data File/EHRI-SDM; U.S. Office of Personnel Management, "Pay Structure of the Federal Civil Service."

Figure 3-3. Change in Federal Employment by Occupational Category, 1973–2014

Percent

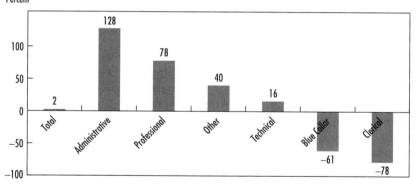

Source: U.S. Office of Personnel Management, Central Personnel Data File/EHRI-SDM.

who guarded the facility during my visit? A private contractor: Wackenhut.

The shift in the federal budget toward more entitlements and the shift of more federal action through proxies like private contractors put the federal government on a different path from state and local

Figure 3-4. Changes in Employment by Sector (Controlling for Population)

Percent

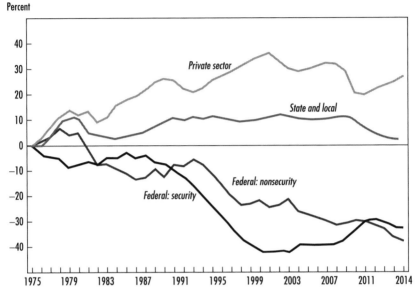

Source: OMB, *Budget of the United States Government, Fiscal Year 2016: Analytical Perspectives* (2015), p. 76 (www.whitehouse.gov/sites/default/files/omb/budget/fy2016/assets/ap _8_strengthening.pdf).
Notes: Federal agencies exclude the military and Postal Service. Security agencies include the Department of Defense, the Department of Homeland Security, the Department of State, and the Department of Veterans Affairs. Nonsecurity agencies include the remainder of the executive branch. State and local agencies exclude educational workers.

governments. At the subnational level, most services are direct, for police, fire, sanitation, and highways. The amount of spending per employee has not varied much. At the federal level, however, each bureaucrat increasingly leverages far more money, because more of the money they manage is going for entitlements and contracts. That explains the shift in the composition of the federal workforce, as well, with fewer employees (especially blue collar and clerical) on the front lines and more managing proxies (as administrators and professionals).

Since 1975, government employment has lagged private sector employment, even after controlling for increases in population. State and local employment has grown slightly, which is not surprising because population growth requires more teachers, police officers, firefighters, and sanitation workers. Federal employment has declined relative to the population, in both national security and other areas. Private sector employment, meanwhile, has grown significantly (see figure 3-4).

LEVERAGING MONEY

The big story overall is that federal employment has hovered around two million workers, but spending, after inflation, has risen sharply (see figure 3-5). The same number of federal employees is leveraging an ever-growing amount of money. It takes a relatively small number of bureaucrats to send a large number of checks. Some entitlement programs, such as Medicare and Medicaid, have complex administrative structures in which employees write regulations for what expenditures

Figure 3-5. Federal Spending and Executive Branch Employment

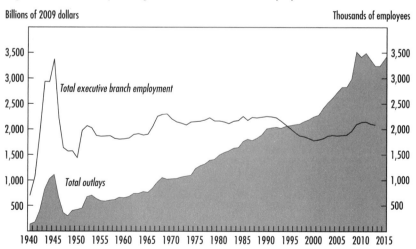

Source: U.S. Office of Personnel Management (http://goo.gl/6iDh0R); U.S. Office of Management and Budget, Historical Tables (www.whitehouse.gov/omb/budget/Historicals).

are eligible and manage financial intermediaries in the private sector, who deal with most of the service providers. Here again, the strategy has been to vastly enlarge the programs without growing the number of government employees.

Over the long haul, from 1940 to 2010, each federal employee on average was increasingly responsible for more money, even after accounting for inflation. Average federal spending per employee, in 2009 dollars, grew exponentially in both defense and civilian programs—but the rate of increase was much faster in civilian programs, as figure 3-6 shows. This is a direct result of the federal government's increasing use of proxies, as more of its work was done outside the federal government—and by the accelerating underinvestment in the people needed to do the work.

In 2013 federal executive branch employment was almost precisely what it was in 1973, at just less than 2.1 million. After 1973 employ-

Figure 3-6. Leveraging Federal Spending

Millions of 2009 dollars per employee

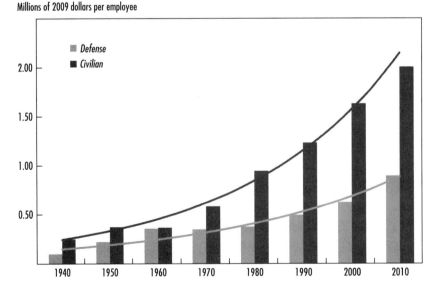

Source: OPM, Historical Federal Workforce Tables, and OMB, Historical Tables.

ment in defense flattened out and then declined. Employment in the civilian agencies meanwhile rose. And the decline in defense employment (30.8 percent) almost precisely matched the rise in employment in the civilian agencies (31.6 percent). Could this be the result of the exploding spending on entitlements? The answer turns out to be no: Employment grew in the Department of Health and Human Services, the Department of Education, and Social Security (but only by 9 percent, compared with the increase in federal spending for entitlements, which grew by more than five times). Employment in defense declined more than any other major federal function, followed by job losses in transportation (17 percent), agriculture (16 percent), and interior (4 percent). Employment in the Treasury grew 24 percent, mainly in the IRS. Jobs serving veterans increased 63 percent, in justice by 170 percent, and in homeland security by 562 percent, mainly as a result of federalizing airport screeners after the September 11 terrorist attacks (see figure 3-7).

Figure 3-7. Changes in Federal Civilian Employment, 1973–2013

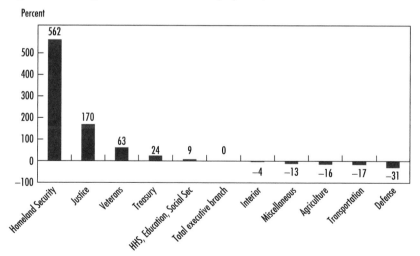

Source: U.S. Office of Personnel Management, *Historical Federal Workforce Tables: Executive Branch Civilian Employment Since 1940* (https://goo.gl/U4VZGc).

This underlines the fundamental trend: The execution of federal programs is increasingly interwoven into the very fabric of the non-governmental world. The degree of interweaving, moreover, varies tremendously by agency. As figure 3-8 shows, some agencies that directly provide goods and services, like the Bureau of the Census, the Transportation Security Agency, and the Veterans Health Administration, have relatively more employees for their budget. The same is true for many regulatory agencies, like the Food and Drug Administration, most of whose budget goes to pay the salary of its workers. For agencies that run transfer programs, such as the IRS (with its tax credit programs), the Social Security Administration, the Office of Personnel Management (with its retirement programs for federal employees), and the Centers for Medicare and Medicaid Services (CMS), a tiny number of employees leverage vast sums of money. In fact, CMS leverages more than 3,000 times as much money per employee as the Bureau of the Census does. Thus, not only is interweaving widespread; the degree of interweaving varies greatly through the federal government, with a handful of agencies responsible for a truly enormous leverage of federal resources. Even in regulatory agencies like the FDA, however, the decisions by small numbers of administrators leverage vast amounts of private sector activity. There is no drug or medical device on the market that does not have the FDA's imprint on it.

In brief, the government conducts an increasing amount of its work through tools interwoven with other sectors, as we will explore in more detail in chapter 4. This interwoven work is inherently more complicated than direct administration. It is more prone to the risks of fraud, waste, abuse, and mismanagement; harder to manage; and harder to hold accountable. That does not necessarily make it worse than governance that relies on more traditional tools—just harder. And the more that government disinvests in its own capacity, the more likely these hard puzzles will lead to bigger problems.

Figure 3-8. Federal Employees' Leverage over the Budget

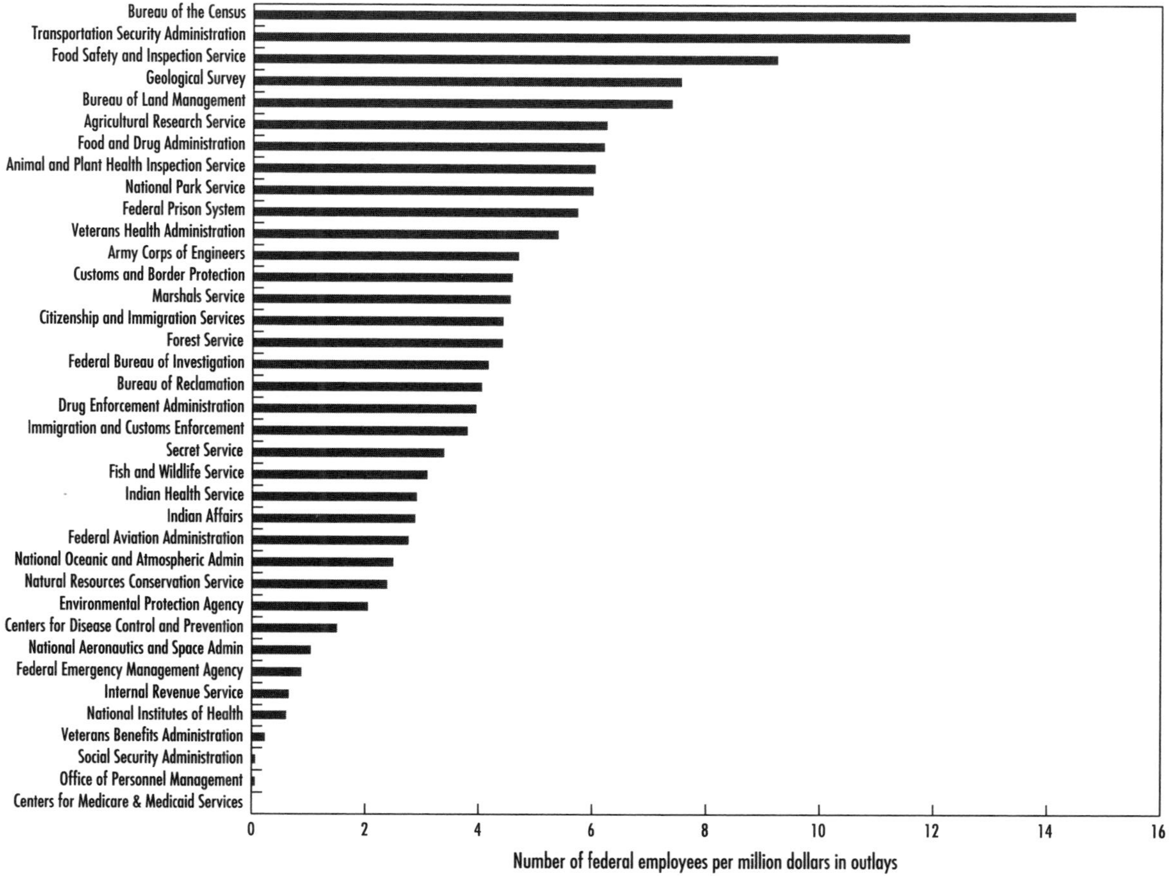

Bureau of the Census
Transportation Security Administration
Food Safety and Inspection Service
Geological Survey
Bureau of Land Management
Agricultural Research Service
Food and Drug Administration
Animal and Plant Health Inspection Service
National Park Service
Federal Prison System
Veterans Health Administration
Army Corps of Engineers
Customs and Border Protection
Marshals Service
Citizenship and Immigration Services
Forest Service
Federal Bureau of Investigation
Bureau of Reclamation
Drug Enforcement Administration
Immigration and Customs Enforcement
Secret Service
Fish and Wildlife Service
Indian Health Service
Indian Affairs
Federal Aviation Administration
National Oceanic and Atmospheric Admin
Natural Resources Conservation Service
Environmental Protection Agency
Centers for Disease Control and Prevention
National Aeronautics and Space Admin
Federal Emergency Management Agency
Internal Revenue Service
National Institutes of Health
Veterans Benefits Administration
Social Security Administration
Office of Personnel Management
Centers for Medicare & Medicaid Services

Number of federal employees per million dollars in outlays

Source: U.S. Office of Management and Budget, *Budget of the United States Government, Fiscal Year 2015: Analytical Perspectives* (2014), table 29-1; U.S. Office of Personnel Management, *FedScope* (www.fedscope.opm.gov).

THE CENTRAL ROLE OF PEOPLE

Since World War II, the complexity of federal programs, coupled with the larger leveraging of federal spending by each employee, has imposed new demands on bureaucrats. The capacity of the federal government to meet these demands, however, has not kept pace. Even after accounting for the rise of entitlement spending and for the rate of inflation, spending grew much faster than the number of feds in place to manage it. Performance problems are piling up. It is impossible to escape the conclusion that government has a serious people problem. Recovering America's lost commitment to competence has to begin by right-sizing the government workforce, and federal employees are simply stretched too thin.

These are big problems that need to be solved. What solutions are most likely to work? A careful reading of GAO's analysis of its high-risk areas reveals a core collection of issues (see figure 3-9). Every program on the list showed problems in managing boundaries—across agencies (at the same level of government), levels of government (including state and local governments), sectors (including links to the private and nonprofit worlds), and nations (including international collaboration). Most programs struggled to set good metrics for measuring results. There were explicit problems in human capital, information management, and technology systems for nearly half of the programs. All of these problems challenged the Progressive consensus of competence, built on a strong government held accountable within strong boundaries. Over time, policy strategies and administrative tactics have fallen further out of sync with the capacity needed to make these programs work. Nowhere has the gap been greater than in its commitment to hiring the right people, with the right skills, in the right places at the right time.

This is true of many more programs than those in GAO's high-risk list, from the far-reaching (like cybersecurity) to the proudly local (like Maryland crab cakes). In 2015 a report by the environmental

Figure 3-9. Common Problems in Risky Programs

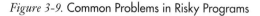

Number of federal employees per million dollars in outlays

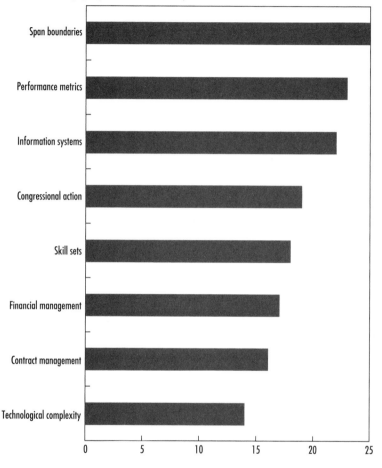

Source: Author's analysis of GAO's 2015 high-risk programs.

interest group Oceana revealed problems that, for many Marylanders, constituted a genuine crisis. Many of the crab cakes sold in Maryland restaurants that were advertised as made from genuine Chesapeake Bay blue crabs were, in fact, mislabeled. DNA testing of the crab cakes found that, instead of containing crab from the bay, 38 percent of the crab cakes were made from imported seafood, including 46 percent in Baltimore and 47 percent in Annapolis, right on the shore of the Chesapeake.[7] How could this have happened? Restaurants bought the crab they could get, and there were not enough government inspectors to keep the advertising honest. The crab cake embarrassment was a people problem at its core.

A different people problem cropped up in Dallas, where the IRS's supervisory revenue officer told a reporter that the agency would not track down those who owed less than $1 million in unpaid taxes. "I have to say, sorry, we can't get that money," explained Richard Christian. "Nobody's ever going to knock on their door." Why? Budget cuts left the agency without 5,000 revenue agents it needed. As a result, $2 billion in taxes went uncollected.[8] At the VA, other people problems surfaced. A year after revelations that veterans were not getting care, and a year after Congress poured in billions of dollars of new money and insisted that the department's secretary be replaced, the wait time for appointments had not budged. In fact, 894,000 appointments took longer than the VA's target of 30 days to schedule, and the number of appointments where the wait was longer than 90 days had nearly doubled.[9]

The examples stretch on, and they share a common theme. Too often, things that Americans want are not getting done and the reason, too often, is a mismatch between the job and the people needed to do it. But it is certainly not a hopeless cause. If GAO's high-risk list documents the worst of the worst, smart federal managers have actually achieved great success in getting their programs off the list. In the first 25 years of the high-risk list, 23 programs have escaped because as a result of the improvements their managers have made. In the savings and loan crisis of the 1980s, the federal government acquired the assets of hundreds of savings and loans, but it paid off the insurance due to depositors, liquidated the assets (which at one time included a Nevada bordello, frozen buffalo semen, and a large stake in the Dallas Cowboys), and closed the federal agency that had been created to do the job (which proved that government agencies do not have an eternal life).[10] The feds vastly improved the management of the Customs Service, the Federal Aviation Administration, and the Forest Service, and they revamped the security clearance process of the Department of Defense. What were the keys to success? What worked, GAO found, was strong leadership commitment, investment in the capacity needed to get the job done, careful monitoring of results, and a commitment to stay with the problems until they were solved. Investment in government's capacity, and careful attention to key details, demonstrated that failure is not the only option. But success builds on people power.

The more complex the world and our government become, the more important government's person power is in delivering the results everyone expects. No one wants to drink foul and dangerous water, deny veterans the health care they have earned through their service, risk homeland security, mismanage defense contracts, or subject Medicare and Medicaid to the dangers of fraud. Smart managers, equipped with the right skills and put in the right place at the right time, are the key to making government work as we all expect it should. Failing to invest in the right people for the right job is the surest path to government waste—and there is no bigger waste in government than failing to deliver on the promises government makes.

BUILDING PEOPLE POWER

It is clear that 21st-century government is not on a hopeless quest to solve its toughest problems, like Don Quixote dreaming the impossible dream. But it is equally clear that government is not performing as it should: Problems pop up more often than they ought to, the costs of poor performance mount, and failures to perform cost money and trust. And although it is impossible to measure, there is a troubling sense that the gap between government's promises and its performance is growing. As problems multiply, the costs escalate. At the very least, intense rapid-fire media coverage puts a harsh and unforgiving light on the problems, and the style of media scrutiny tends to make the problems even harder to solve.

Make no mistake: This is a moment much like the one the first group of Progressives faced in the late 1800s, which they addressed by inventing the Progressive movement's commitment to competence. We need now a new plan to match government's capacity to the strategies it is developing to attack 21st-century problems. Its foundation is people power. Let us break down what this means.

Talent gaps in key areas

It is not just that we do not have enough government employees. We do not have enough of the right employees in the right areas. The problem, the Office of Management and Budget (OMB) concludes, is this: "Federal jobs that have become increasingly complex and require greater levels of skill." As a result, "federal jobs are concentrated in higher paying professions" and require workers with "more high-level degrees."[11] Table 3-1 makes the point clearly about the high levels of talent that the federal government employs. More than half of the federal government's workforce is in the highest-paid occupations, compared with about a third of the private sector workforce.

That conclusion rankles many on the right, who have long believed that government is an entrepreneurial backwater and that the nation's best talent ought to be in the private sector, where new ideas can generate new jobs. A former Office of Personnel Management official in the Reagan administration wrote bluntly in a 1986 *Wall Street Journal* op-ed that it was important to recognize "the private sector as the true vehicle for prosperity, social cohesiveness and national welfare, and as the place where we ought to encourage our best and brightest minds to migrate." The federal government, he contended, "should be content to lure competent people, not the best and most talented people," because "those individuals are needed in the private sector where wealth is produced rather than consumed."[12]

Table 3-1. Federal and Private Sector Workforces

	Percent	
	FEDERAL WORKERS	PRIVATE WORKERS
Highest-paid occupations *Lawyers, engineers, scientists,* *managers, pilots, health care* *workers, administrators, inspectors*	55.6	35.2
Medium-paid occupations *Sales, mechanics, law enforcement,* *office workers, drivers, laborers,* *clerks, manufacturing*	40.0	52.3
Lowest-paid occupations *Service workers, janitors,* *housekeepers, cooks, wait staff*	4.4	12.4

Source: Office of Management and Budget, *Budget of the United States Government, Fiscal Year 2016: Analytical Perspectives*, 2015, p. 78 (www.whitehouse.gov/sites/default/files/omb/budget/fy2016/assets/ap_8_strengthening.pdf).

The growing paradox, however, of pushing talent from government into the private sector is that so much of the private sector's business now depends on government, especially through contracts. Government failures can punish private partners severely, especially if government proves not a very good partner to work with. Moreover, government is so interwoven into the private and nonprofit sectors, as we will see in chapter 4, that citizens and companies alike depend on government to maintain stable markets. Without sufficient talent, government becomes error-prone and the mistakes ripple throughout society, sometimes with rapid and enormous consequences, not only for public services but also for the private economy.

Government has big skill gaps, especially in five areas, as OMB found: cybersecurity, acquisitions and contract management, economics, human resources, and auditing.[13] Building government's capacity in a new Progressive commitment to competence requires plugging the gap between the skills that the government has and the ones it needs to cope with 21st-century problems.

A weak talent development system

As OMB found, "In the past sixty years, the private sector has developed innovative and more flexible personnel management systems, but the Federal personnel system has not kept up."[14] Much of government's people system is a stale vestige of laws that created the current pay system in 1949 and its benefits system in 1951. It was the high-water mark of the Progressive bipartisan coalition, a triumph of a modern government that had fought and won a two-front world war. In 1950 the federal government was vastly different than it was in the first decades of the 21st century. The nation was transitioning from the massive World War II buildup to a new economy with a permanent defense establishment. Social Security was a shadow of its current form, and Medicare and Medicaid lay more than 15 years in the future. The regulatory state had not fully emerged. On average, each federal employee was responsible for $294 million (in 2009 dollars). By 2013 that amount had grown to $1.5 billion, more than a fivefold increase, in a policy world full of proxies and globalized impact.

There is an enormous paradox here. The high-water mark of the Progressive era defined the government's human talent system for more than two generations, from a foundation built at precisely the moment at which the policy underpinnings of the Progressive movement came apart. The strains have grown over time, to the point that, in a statement of clarity unusual for a budget document, OMB concluded in 2015, "Quite simply, a 21st-century Government cannot continue to operate using 20th-century processes."[15]

There is no secret about what needs to be done. Fundamental improvements in government's capacity must begin with crucial improvements in its people systems.[16] The government needs more flexibility to identify talent and recruit effectively for the workers with the skills it needs; it needs a pay and benefits system that is competitive with private markets; it needs a talent management system that rewards top performers and deals with poor performers, including increasing flexibility in firing those whose work is substandard. And as the government workforce ages—the federal workforce is older than the private sector workforce—the government must manage the transition from retiring Baby Boomers to talented Millennials who are seeking paths to have an impact and make a difference.[17]

Even within the antiquated constraints of the current system, the government has shown it can crack some of society's toughest problems. That is the broad story of the success of federal managers in cracking government's toughest problems. It is a fight, but it is worth having—and it must be won.

Little political traction in making the case for people in government

This people piece is, at once, the easiest and toughest one for reclaiming government. It is the easiest piece because the case for investing in people is self-evident, as private sector managers recognize. In fact, "our people are our most important asset" has become such a cliché in the private sector that some authors have taken to throwing occasional rocks at the adage just to be contrarian. But no private sector manager would try to move the organization forward by trashing the people who work for it, as too painfully and too often is the case in government. As I argue throughout this book, the paradox of government's growing complexity is that it has made individual leadership, backed up by data and technology, all the more important.

It is also the toughest piece because making the case for bureaucrats gets little political traction. Liberals have often energetically pressed ahead with their most ambitious programs without thinking about how to manage them. Conservatives have resisted government's expansion by refusing to invest in bureaucrats. From polar-opposite directions, they have found an uneasy political consensus in ignoring, abusing, or underfunding government's capacity. As the ideologies of the Left and the Right ripened at the end of the 20th century, there was little room for figuring out how their plans would work, either the expansion of the social welfare state of the Left or the strong defense establishment of the Right. Performance problems plagued both their houses. GAO's high-risk list, for example, has as many Republican as it has Democratic fingerprints on it.

Nothing makes the case better than the struggle to launch the Affordable Care Act, passed by Congress in 2010. For the Democrats, it was the ultimate triumph of decades of work. Obama succeeded, where Clinton and others had failed, in enacting a comprehensive health insurance program covering all Americans. But when it came time for the program's launch in 2013, its website collapsed and the Obama administration was profoundly embarrassed. The administration had won its ideological victory but stumbled in its practical launch. The Republicans opposed to health insurance reform—as well as those who saw a wonderful opportunity to wound the president—launched recurring attacks on the program's funding. If they could not repeal the law, they intended at least to prevent its effective administration. The result was a law for which there was not political support for repeal and a program that was administratively damaged. It was a premier example of the pathology into which the original Progressive movement had fallen. It was another campaign in the broader battle in which the *how* of policy edged out the political struggles over the *what*.

Government's people system further out of sync with the system we need

America has found itself more or less locked into a government whose capacity to deliver has fallen further out of sync with the demands of governance. For more than a century, Americans took for granted the Progressive approach. It then pressed the movement to its breaking point through the expansion of proxies, without a means to manage them. That worked politically for each party. Democrats could expand their programs without having to take responsibility for the costs of running them well. Republicans could attack bureaucracy without having to give up on programs they wanted to keep. This quiet conspiracy fueled the steady expansion of government's growing ambition that each party, in its own way, supported. Each party took the model for granted—until, that is, the model began crumbling under the weight of the government it helped create.

THE ROLE OF PEOPLE IN RECOVERING GOVERNMENT

We have ended up with a government crippled in its ability to deliver on the promises it makes. Performance problems have fueled each party's tactical attacks on the other. They have also left citizens ever more furious about a government that struggles to deliver. Management failures are driving costs up and citizen trust down. Taking for granted the process of service delivery has become an expensive— and dangerous—instinct. There can be no path to recovering government—and escaping Jurassic government—without building on employees who can lead on the path to excellence.

The biggest challenge for these employees is managing a government increasingly interwoven with nongovernmental partners. We turn to that challenge next.

FOUR

The Rise of Interweaving

IT'S EASY TO SAVAGE GOVERNMENT'S performance along with the
people who manage public programs. Tales of waste, fraud, abuse, and
mismanagement tumble off television screens, newspaper pages, and
online blogs. A Google search for "government waste" turned up nearly
33 million hits, so it is little wonder that political candidates promise
they will cut government and slash waste.

In the litany of stories about waste, it is easy to miss three important threads. One is that government's problems are far more open to
public view than is the case in the private sector. Government's failures spill from the front pages of newspapers and cable news; the private sector's failures are buried in balance sheets that almost no one
reads. Citizens expect transparency in government, from open records and meetings to access to e-mails. Private companies expect precisely the reverse.

The second is that well-run private companies deliberately strategize about how much waste they will accept. Ten percent of the food cooked in fast-food restaurants ends up in the trash instead of being served to customers because it does not meet corporate standards for freshness. After seven minutes, McDonald's restaurants throw out their fries. If they sit longer, the company calculates, they just would not taste like McDonald's fries.[1] During the construction of the twin towers of the World Trade Center in New York during the early 1970s, the glass covers for light fixtures on several floors were tossed into dumpsters because they did not fit. (I did some of the dumpster tossing.) Sometimes private companies explicitly calculate how much waste they will accept in exchange for the quality of services they want to provide. Sometimes they simply make mistakes and bury the expense in their accounts. It is a separate, debatable, and ultimately unknowable question about whether waste in government is greater than in the private sector, but it is surely not the case that the private sector is free from significant waste.

The third and most important thread is this: Government tends to do the things that the private sector cannot or will not. The government's complex tools often make public programs inherently harder to manage. It also makes it all the more remarkable that so much of government works so well so often. Consider this quick checklist:

—*Air safety.* Federal Aviation Administration controllers guide more than 25 million flights per year from their gates at the terminal through takeoff and landing and then on to their arrival gates.[2] That works out to 869 billion revenue passenger miles (the number of passengers paying to fly and the distance they travel). The radar-driven minuet around major airports is simply remarkable. The FAA's work, combined with the research of the National Transportation Safety Board, has dramatically improved air safety by making planes far more sturdy and reliable.

—*Social Security.* More than 59 million Americans get monthly retirement payments from the agency. The accuracy is so high that the error rate barely registers.

—*Highway safety.* In 1994, 40,716 Americans died in traffic accidents. In 2012 the number dropped 18 percent, to 33,561. Of course, in the meantime, more Americans are driving more miles. The fatality rate is down 32 percent; per mile, the rate dropped 35 percent.[3] This is the result of government work at all levels: stronger federal regulations by the National Highway Traffic Safety Administration and better highway design through a partnership of federal, state, and local government officials.

—*Air quality.* Since 1980 air quality has improved dramatically. Lead in the air is down 92 percent, carbon monoxide is down 84 percent, and ozone (a main ingredient of smog) is down 33 percent, thanks to the work of the U.S. Environmental Protection Agency and its state counterparts.[4] Residents of Los Angeles have rediscovered what the surrounding mountains look like.

—*Fire deaths.* Local firefighters and stronger building codes have greatly reduced the consequences of fires. The number of fires declined 19.5 percent from 2002 to 2011. Deaths dropped 20.6 percent, and property loss diminished 4.3 percent.[5] Moreover, for every fire call the local fire department responds to, there are nearly seven calls for emergency medical assistance and rescue.

All of these are things that citizens expect government to do. All of them are good things. None of them is easy to do. And none of them would have happened without government.

Government often ends up with jobs that citizens want done but that the private sector cannot or will not do. In some cases, that work must undo the problems caused by the private sector. There is an eternal battle over just where to draw the line on government's power, but there is no question that government does a lot, that citizens want government to do most of it, and that much of what it does is difficult.

Government is increasingly doing these things through tools interwoven with the private and nonprofit sectors, in ways that complicate the Progressive commitment to competence that emerged over the preceding century—and that confound the foundations of accountability on which the growth of government's power was built.

DOING HARD THINGS IN HARD WAYS

The government's ever-growing mission has its roots in the Constitution, just 21 words into its preamble. The founders committed the new government to "provide for the common defence" and "promote the general Welfare." The Constitution's provision for a federal post office led to the construction of post roads. The opportunity to purchase Louisiana—actually, an enormous swath of America's middle from New Orleans to Montana—made Thomas Jefferson, the most Jeffersonian of limited-government advocates, into a strong-executive Hamiltonian.

In the nation's early decades, however, government's reach was relatively limited. Private turnpikes, operated as toll roads, dominated interstate commerce for the nation's first generation, until private wooden plank roads replaced them. Government was relatively small through the first half of the 19th century, at about 2 percent of the gross domestic product. The major exceptions were during wartime— about 3 percent during the War of 1812, and 13 percent in 1865 at the height of the Civil War, a level it would not see again until World War I and would not permanently surpass until 1948 (see figure 4-1).

In fact, the story of federal spending is not one of steady, inexorable growth. Rather, it is the tale of a ratchet: Government operated on a plateau until interrupted by war, after which spending found a new level, lower than the intensive activity during wartime but higher than in prewar days (see figure 4-2). Even in the volatile post–World War II decades, with wars in Korea, Vietnam, Iraq, and Afghanistan— and with wars on poverty, pollution, and terror—federal spending

Figure 4-1. Federal Spending as a Percentage of GDP

Percent of GDP

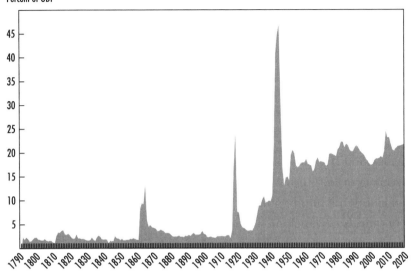

Source: USGovernmentSpending.com (www.usgovernmentspending.com/spending_chart
_1792_2020USp_16s1li011mcn_F0t).

hovered around 19 percent of GDP. Behind this growth are two important and interesting questions: how to empower government without fueling tyranny, and once the federal government's spending plateaued at about 19 percent of GDP, how to continue extending its reach. The plateaus are built not only on a growing government role but also, at each step, on an increasing reliance of government on nongovernmental actors to get its work done.

Every American knows about Patrick Henry's speech to the Virginia Convention in 1775. "Gentlemen may cry, Peace, Peace—but there is no peace. The war is actually begun!" he told his fellow Virginians. Others might debate the right course, "but as for me, give me liberty or give me death!"[6] The pursuit of liberty not only fueled the revolution, it also set the basic strategy for governance for the new country, with just enough government to keep the peace but not so

Figure 4-2. Average Government Peacetime Spending

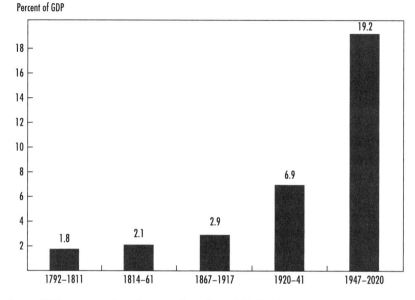

Percent of GDP

Source: USGovernmentSpending.com (http://goo.gl/I2oFnA).

much government as to restrain commerce. Since then, the American story has been a consistent expansion of government's role—and, as that role has expanded, a constant battle has raged to control government's growing power. Most other industrialized nations have not had this struggle because they do not share the deep, abiding fear that so many Americans have about government's role. With the rise of their welfare states, they expanded their government's role much more, and much more directly. The United States has been different. It is average in size, but its reach has extended ever more deeply into the nongovernmental sectors, through tools that blur the central question of who is responsible for doing what. This "government by proxy," as I have called it, has increasingly defined how government does what it does—especially how it has grown.[7] First, however, came the Progressive consensus that made government's growth possible.

THE RISE OF THE PROGRESSIVE CONSENSUS

The country grew economically on the base of liberty that the founders built. The Civil War established the federal government's primacy, and that in turn became the foundation on which the modern American state grew.

In the latter part of the 19th century, the Progressive consensus fundamentally transformed government's role. That revolution did not come through a vast increase in government spending. Federal *spending* increased a bit, but the real story was the growth of the federal government's *reach*, fueled by the Progressives' conviction that private power was poisoning public life and that the government needed more power to rein it in.

In the late 1800s, muckrakers found plenty of muck to rake. They pointed to corporate monopolies, which built huge empires at the expense of consumers. They wrote about the unimaginable conditions that immigrants suffered in the nation's urban slums and the horrific treatment of animals in the nation's food chain. Most of all, they pointed to the political corruption that flowed from unchecked corporate power. Through their exposés, Jacob Riis, Upton Sinclair, and Ida Tarbell became household names.[8] They made the case for a stronger governmental reach, far deeper into the operations of the private sector. At the highest levels, however, government officials worried about this expansion of government's power. As he considered the proposal creating the Interstate Commerce Commission, designed to rein in railroad monopolies, President Grover Cleveland was quoted as saying that he "did not believe it was ever intended that Government should continually interfere with business," and that he was greatly concerned that "the use by independent bodies of the authority of the executive, whether in nation or state, should enable them to concentrate into their hands the great enterprizes [*sic*] of the country." But Cleveland recognized that "there were abuses and grievances which demanded correction" and signed the bill "in spite of reservations."[9]

The path to the Progressives was not an easy one, especially given the nation's traditional aversion to strong government and its instinct to allow citizens—and the companies they created—substantial freedom. The rise of corporate monopolies and the problems they created, however, laid the foundation for changing that. And with that not only came the rise of the Progressive movement but also the creation of the modern American state.

How could government's power grow without creating a government that was tyrannical? In 1887 a promising Princeton University political scientist, Woodrow Wilson, proposed an answer, before moving from professor to president. He believed that the best management ideas from the world of business could be brought to government, but with managerial power held strictly accountable to elected officials. "If I see a murderous fellow sharpening a knife cleverly," he wrote, "I can borrow his way of sharpening the knife without borrowing his probable intent to commit murder with it." Government administration could professionalize without becoming politicized. The key, he argued, was keeping administration separate from politics but holding it under tight political control.[10]

The birth of the modern American state came with the Progressives and, in particular, the creation of the civil service in 1883. In the 1880 presidential campaign, Ohio Republican James Garfield faced Winfield Hancock from Pennsylvania. A relatively unsuccessful lawyer, Charles Guiteau, gave a couple of speeches to support Garfield. The Ohioan won an easy victory, but Guiteau convinced himself that his speeches had turned the tide and that he deserved a major position. The post of ambassador to France, he concluded, would be just right. White House aides shunned Guiteau, along with most of the office seekers who lined up every day looking for jobs in the new administration. At that point, federal jobs went to loyalists, and elections brought floods of new officials, from high to low, to Washington. Furious at the slight, Guiteau decided to exact revenge by shooting the president at the Baltimore and Potomac railroad station in

Washington, where the West Building of the National Gallery of Art is now located. One bullet lodged deep in the president's torso. After lingering for almost three months, the president died just ten months after taking office.

Reformers, led by Ohio Democratic Senator George H. Pendleton, decided that the revolving door of patronage appointments in the executive branch had to stop. In 1883 they passed the Civil Service Reform Act, which required federal bureaucrats to be hired on the basis of merit, not politics. Jobs were defined by classification, according to what the jobholder needed to know, not by the person who held the job. Hiring and promotion were to be based on objective measures, not a supervisor's discretion. And government employment was to be a career, not a temporary service limited by the term of a political patron. It was a showcase for the idea of borrowing professional management from the private sector but holding it strictly accountable.

The Pendleton Act created strong power within tight boundaries. It framed the model for the theory of *how* a larger, more ambitious, more professional American government was to be run. Indeed, by creating the modern American bureaucracy it was midwife to the modern American administrative state. Civil service reform was about process, but the same model was applied to new structures, especially independent regulatory agencies with great power but greater insulation from political pressures because they were created outside cabinet departments. Congress passed laws to create the Interstate Commerce Commission (1887) to rein in the railroads. The Food and Drug Administration (1906) oversaw the safety of the food chain and consumer products. The Federal Reserve (1913) reduced the wild economic swings that private bankers inflicted on the economy, and the Federal Trade Commission (1914) worked to bust monopolies. It was the Progressive revolution, which answered Cleveland's dilemma on how to solve public problems without excessively interfering with business. The answer built on Wilson's notion of empowering bureaucrats but holding them accountable, separating their professional role from political power. Despite the notion of liberal Democratic big-government power that came to flavor Progressivism toward the end of the 20th century, this strategy was remarkably bipartisan. And so strongly were Americans anchored to it that they continued to rely on the theory even after the practice began to drift from these foundations. Indeed, the story of 20th-century government in the United States is the continued growth of government, the continued reliance on the Progressive ideal to keep it competent and accountable, a growing drift of the actual practice of government away from that Progressive ideal, and an ever-widening gap between the demands of governmental programs and government's capacity to manage them well. It was the path by which Progressivism became Jurassic.

PROGRESSIVISM BECOMES JURASSIC

The Great Depression challenged the foundations of the Progressive movement. Herbert Hoover's efforts to rely primarily on private markets and to nudge them back on track had not worked, and the country was desperate for far more aggressive action. As he took office, Franklin D. Roosevelt faced a tough dilemma: How could he expand government's role and reach without further undermining private markets—and eroding the very foundation of the guiding public philosophy that had made an expansion of governmental power possible?

His answer was a hybrid version of the Progressive movement, with new government tools and fuzzier boundaries controlling them. He established an alphabet soup of new government agencies, for sure. But more important, he created systems of shared power between the federal government and other players acting on its behalf. He began by pumping federal money into the economy, through a pragmatic brand of Keynesian-like policies before economist John Maynard Keynes wrote his 1936 classic, which argued that government could stimulate the private economy in times of trouble by increasing its spending and running deficits. From 1930 to 1935, government spending as a share of the economy more than doubled, from 4.3 percent to 10.2 percent. A big part of the growth came through the vast expansion of federal grant programs, especially for public works projects. From just 1930 to 1935, intergovernmental aid grew sixfold, from 0.2 percent of GDP to 1.3 percent.

This was a fundamental shift in governance. Rather than having the federal government do the job itself, federal grants created incentives for state and local governments to act through federal money they could not refuse for programs they were induced to pursue. It provided a strategy for expanding the federal government's power without the government's doing the work itself. And while defense spending squeezed out federal spending for grants during World War II, it exploded in the postwar years. The strategy funded urban renewal and the federal government's 90 percent share of the interstate highway system. Federal grants funded a major portion of urban renewal and Medicaid, the federal government's program to fund health and long-term care expenses for the poor and the elderly (see figure 4-3). In 1987 federal grants for payments to individuals—mostly for Medicaid—exceeded all other federal grants. That shift continued until, in 2015, grants for payments to individuals amounted to nearly 75 percent of all federal aid.[11]

When World War II broke out, a similar kind of pragmatism emerged in new public-private partnerships. The government needed to gear up—fast—to fight a two-front war. Rather than do the work itself, it did what it had always done in wartime—rely on private contractors—but this time it was on a vastly larger scale. It did not use contractors just to produce rations and uniforms and planes and rifles. The most sensitive wartime weapon, the atomic bomb, emerged from a highly compartmentalized network of government-owned, contractor-operated facilities, from the Oak Ridge National Laboratory in Tennessee, where researchers demonstrated that they could extract weapons-grade plutonium, to the Hanford Site in Washington,

Figure 4-3. Federal Grants to State and Local Governments as a Percentage of GDP

Percent of GDP

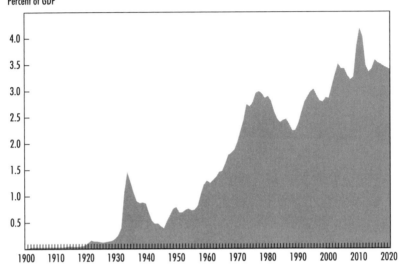

Source: USGovernmentSpending.com (http://goo.gl/p6QE3w).

where workers built reactors to extract plutonium for bombs. The military also relied heavily on contractors in the actual theater of fighting, at three times the rate of contracting during World War I. The role of contractors in the military theater tripled yet again in fighting the Korean War, with an even larger ratio of contractors to military personnel. During the war in the Balkans in the 1990s and the war in Iraq in the 2000s, the military's reliance on in-theater contractors nearly tripled again, with one contractor for every member of the armed forces in the field (see figure 4-4).

The rising role of both grants and contracts departed significantly from the dominant philosophy of the Progressives: instead of expanding governmental power within tight boundaries, to hold it accountable, and building new systems to advance competence, these tools pushed the federal government past its organizational silos into partnerships with other levels of government, with private companies, and

Figure 4-4. Ratio of Government Contractors to Military Personnel: 20th-Century Military Operations

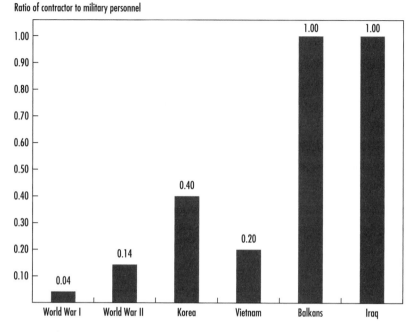

Ratio of contractor to military personnel

Source: Congressional Budget Office, *Contractors' Support of U.S. Operations in Iraq* (Washington, D.C., 2008), p. 13 (www.cbo.gov/sites/default/files/08-12-iraqcontractors.pdf).

increasingly with nonprofit organizations. The new tools required different management to be used well but, as the government developed them, there was no explicit recognition of the new capacity needed. Government continued to grow, but without careful thought about how to hold it accountable or make it effective. Even worse, it began straying down the Jurassic road. It used the Progressive approach to the philosophy of government without building post-Progressive tools to manage the programs that the old approach did not fit. The result was a gradually emerging gap between the goals of government and the strategies to manage it well—and, as the commitment to competence eroded and performance problems rose, there was a gradual fraying of the Progressive consensus.

This strategy of interweaving expanded in the postwar years, with even more new federal grant programs to state and local governments, from building interstate highways to waging war on poverty. And the expansion did not stop there. The federal government created new lending programs, both through loans made directly by the government and loans government guaranteed or subsidized (or both) through private lenders. Consider the federal Direct Student Loan program, created in 1993 to help students fund higher education, after several decades of expanding federal support. Student borrowing increased at a remarkable rate, until in 2010 student debt surpassed borrowing for auto loans and credit cards (see figure 4-5). Federal lending grew in areas as far-ranging as housing, clean energy, business development, and international development. The federal government also insures bank deposits and private pensions. It administers a national flood insurance program for homeowners whose properties lie in harm's way and a crop insurance program for farmers who sometimes face harsh weather. Congress established insurance programs to cover losses from terrorism and war risk to airline companies. The direct loans from the government and loans made by private lenders that the government guarantees vastly expanded. The federal government does not just provide goods and services. It has become one of the world's largest banks (see figure 4-6).

The loan programs created strong incentives and inadvertently produced large impacts, both in how much government was committed to spend and what kind of debt students incurred. From 1993 through 2012, both the number and debt burden of graduates carrying student loans totaling more than $100,000 grew significantly, especially for students who went on to graduate school in medicine and law (figure 4-7; see page 83). Federal loan programs inadvertently became a subsidy program for students going into relatively well-paying professions. Moreover, the availability of student loans made it easy for these graduate programs to raise tuition, since the government

Figure 4-5. Increase in Student Loan Market

Trillions of dollars

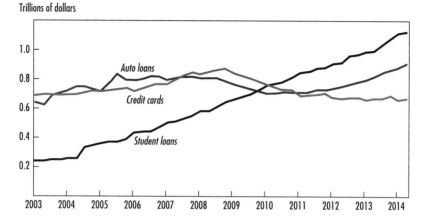

Source: Ericka Davis, "Student Debt: Trends and Possible Consequences," *Financial Insights* 3, no. 3 (2014) (www.dallasfed.org/assets/documents/banking/firm/fi/fi1403.pdf).

Figure 4-6. Federal Credit Outstanding

Trillions of dollars

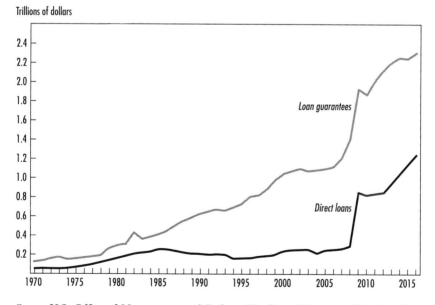

Source: U.S. Office of Management and Budget, "Credit and Insurance," *Budget of the United States Government: Fiscal Year 2016—Analytical Perspectives* (Washington, D.C., 2015), p. 322 (www.whitehouse.gov/sites/default/files/omb/budget/fy2016/assets/ap_20 _credit.pdf).

proved a handy bank for financing and subsidizing it. Along the way, the federal government created a contingent repayment program, which forgave student loan debt for graduates who went to work in public service careers. This created further incentives for students to load up on debt, because the federal government would write much of it off in time, and it encouraged even more tuition increases. And then, when the media began playing stories about students acquiring (and being forgiven) large loans, political support for the programs began to erode, and that threatened to jeopardize federal support for student loans in general.

In the absence of a broad policy—and any policy debate—the federal government found itself pouring enormous resources into graduate education and rewarding the students who borrowed most profligately. For the area in which the government itself needed the most help—building a generation of students who could help lead government effectively in the post-Progressive programs—the government had neither a solid loan program nor a sound strategy for hiring the students it most needed. The loan programs were attractive politics, for they allowed the government to help without putting the programs on the budget. But they proved bad policy by putting enormous amounts of taxpayer dollars at risk and failing to recruit the people the government needed most. It proved the poster child of a policy that emerged as the Progressive philosophy lost its Progressive commitment to competence.

The federal government also leveraged private action through tax deductions and tax credits administered through the tax code. In the United Kingdom, the government is phasing out the annual process of citizens' filling out tax returns. The U.K. government will create a tax account for each citizen, and taxpayers will spend just ten minutes a year checking the account to ensure all is in order. For most American taxpayers, such a system would be impossible. That is not because the technology is not there. Because of the wide variety of American tax breaks, such as the deductions for home mortgage inter-

Figure 4-7. Increase in Student Borrowing for Grad School

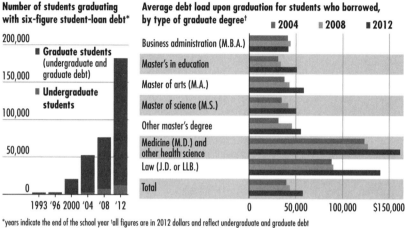

Borrowing for Grad School

Six-figure debts have soared for graduate students, especially those studying to be doctors or lawyers.

Source: Wall Street Journal, August 18, 2015 (www.wsj.com/articles/loan-binge-by-graduate-students-fans-debt-worries-1439951900?mod=djemCapitalJournalDaybreak).

est and property tax and charitable deductions, as well as preferential tax rates for capital gains, American tax returns are inordinately complicated. The IRS estimates that it takes typical taxpayers about 13 hours a year to file their taxes: 4 hours on the forms themselves, and 9 hours to collect the backup paperwork. In contrast, the U.K. government estimates that it will take taxpayers just ten minutes to complete the process.

This contrast is not the result of an all-powerful IRS. It is because the American tax code provides tax breaks that Americans treasure and that Congress will not repeal. These tax breaks have now risen to the point where they equal the federal government's discretionary spending (see figure 4-8). The difference: They are not subject to any regular budgetary review. That, of course, was not what President Warren G. Harding had in mind when he signed the 1921 law that created the annual federal budget process. That budget process helped

Figure 4-8. Tax Expenditures by the Federal Government

Billions of 2013 dollars

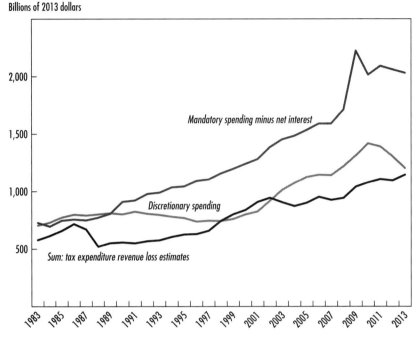

Source: U.S. Government Accountability Office, "Tax Expenditures" (www.gao.gov/key
_issues/tax_expenditures/issue_summary).

strengthen the foundations of Progressivism. The rise of the enormous system of tax preferences has weakened it.

The same is true of government regulations. Everyone complains
about red tape (whose origin lies in the ribbons used to tie up the Civil
War service records of soldiers—to manage pensions, government
clerks would often have to literally cut the red tape). But every rule
and regulation exists for some good reason, at least when it was written, with some important constituency standing behind it who thought
it was a good idea. Those reasons still exist, even if almost everyone
has forgotten about them, and that makes it all the harder to unwind
the regulations on the books. Federal regulations are responsible for
the increase in auto and airline safety, the improvements in environ-

Figure 4-9. Growth of Federal Regulatory Activity

Number of pages in the *Federal Register*

Source: Office of the Federal Register (www.federalregister.gov/uploads/2014/04/OFR -STATISTICS-CHARTS-ALL1-1-1-2013.pdf), in Mave Carey, *Counting Regulations: An Overview of Rulemaking, Types of Federal Regulations, and Pages in the Federal Register* (Washington, D.C.: Congressional Research Service, November 26, 2014), p. 17 (http://fas.org /sgp/crs/misc/R43056.pdf).

mental quality, and the undoubted increased costs and aggravation in dealing with the vast array of government rules. There is no good measure of the volume of federal rules or of their financial burdens. But for a rough measure of the activity around federal rules, see figure 4-9 and the count of pages published annually in the *Federal Register*, the federal government's daily journal of regulatory record. It has greatly increased over the years and accelerated the use of proxies.

THE PROGRESSIVE MOVEMENT IN DISARRAY

For more than a century, Republicans and Democrats embraced the Progressive movement and its strategy for growing government while holding it accountable. As new problems arose and government rose to address them, they managed to convince themselves that they were remaining true to the fundamental principles constraining the growth of government's power. In reality, they embraced what was convenient—the case for bigger government—without accepting its guiding principles of competence and accountability.

It was perfectly understandable, since the guiding principles proved politically convenient for Republicans and Democrats alike. They provided a pragmatic road on which both parties could ride their plans for ever-more-expansive public programs. However, by the end of the 20th century the movement was in disarray, because the gap between the underlying principles and the pragmatic realities of making those programs work had reached the breaking point. The more government programs expanded without devising a strategy to manage them and the more they became interwoven, the more problems of performance and accountability deepened—the very problems that the Progressive movement was originally invented to solve back in the 19th century.

This gradual evolution not only changed the way the government worked, it transformed the financial foundations of many of the government's partners. Many large private companies, especially in the space and defense world, would be shadows of themselves without government contracts. When Edward Snowden leaked massive amounts of classified data about the National Security Agency's activities in 2012, the controversy cast a sharp light on an important side issue. Snowden was not an employee of the NSA but of the consulting firm Booz Allen Hamilton, which provided work—including Snowden's—under contract to the NSA. Booz Allen Hamilton, in turn, was one of the federal government's largest contractors, with $4 billion in federal government business that year. The contracts accounted for 99 percent of the company's revenue.[12]

It is impossible to readily determine how much of a foundation government contracts provide for most government contractors—most of that information is either held closely or buried in the companies' annual reports—but the Snowden case is just one sign of how interwoven governmental work has become in the business of private companies. And this is not just the case for private companies. In 2011 grants and contracts from governments accounted for a third of all revenues for public charities, more than twice what they raised from individual donors.[13] State and local governments have become increasingly dependent on federal cash. In 2010 federal grants accounted for more than one of every three dollars that state and local governments spent from their own sources (37.5 percent), up from 25.2 percent in 1990.[14]

PATTERNS OF INTERWEAVING

In doing its work, the federal government depends increasingly on its interwoven partners. The federal government's partners, in turn, depend increasingly on the federal government for their budgets. This is the real issue hiding behind the battle over government's size. The growth of its power has not come so much through the number of its own employees but through the increasing weaving of its operations in a nongovernmental fabric of contractors, in both the private and nonprofit sectors. That has broadened its reach and deepened its grasp on a vast range of American society. The interweaving grew from the Progressives' roots, but it has emerged in a form that the original Progressives, Republicans and Democrats alike, would simply not recognize.

Between government agencies

Some of this interweaving is *internal* to government. It is rare that managing a government program does not involve an interagency working group, because responsibility for almost every governmental program flows over agency boundaries. Barack Obama tried to make a joke of the boundary issues in his 2011 State of the Union address, where he pointed out that 12 different agencies deal with export policies and five oversee housing programs. His favorite, he said, was the management of fisheries. "The Interior Department is in charge of salmon while they're in fresh water, but the Commerce Department handles them when they're in salt water," he said. "I hear it gets even more complicated once they're smoked."[15] These government regulations are not set up to confuse the salmon; the boundaries are created to meet the needs of those who fish. Interior manages freshwater salmon because the Fish and Wildlife Service manages the protection and conservation of the fish when they are swimming in rivers and streams, and the service is in the Interior Department. Once they reach open water, the fish swim under the jurisdiction of the National Marine Fisheries Service, which ensures compliance with fishing policy and is in the Commerce Department. The U.S. Department of Agriculture takes over when the fish is smoked and becomes part of the food chain.[16] Different agencies have different jurisdictions because the same salmon raises different policy issues, depending on where they are swimming and who is trying to catch them.

Between levels of government

Other forms of interweaving are *external*, between the federal government and its partners at other levels of government and between government and other sectors of society. The attack of the killer tomatoes—actually, killer peppers—we explored in chapter 3 is, at its core, a case of interweaving among levels of government. Federal agencies had expert help from state officials in Minnesota and county officials in North Carolina, as well as teams from the Arizona and New Mexico state governments and the Navajo Nation. Federal grants for Medicaid fund a partnership with the states for health care focused on the poor. In addition to paying for vaccinations for low-income children and dental care, a third of Medicaid's outlays go for long-term care of the elderly and disabled. The program pays for two-thirds of the cost of all nursing home residents, and, as the number of elderly in the country rises, Medicaid's contribution for long-term care is sure to go up—as is its contribution to the costs of the nursing home industry.[17]

With the private and nonprofit sectors

Government's contracting has been on the increase, not only for defense but also for an array of social service programs. Contractors, whether for-profit or nonprofit, provide most frontline social services, from summer meal programs to job training. Contractors clean government buildings and provide transportation for government employees. They provide advice, from local zoning to cybersecurity. To say that most government employees have become managers of contracted-out services is an exaggeration; we do not have the numbers to know for sure. But it is no exaggeration to say that contractors have become a huge part of the interwoven network of public goods and services, and that government is struggling to build the capacity to keep up.

With foreign stakeholders

Presidents, both Democratic and Republican, have increasingly sought to enlist other nations in military operations, both to gain extra firepower and to build a broader base of political support. When the Great Recession hit in 2008, the government's chief financial officials were constantly on the phone with their international counterparts to coordinate their response. Cyberdefense is increasingly a global effort, but even in relatively mundane issues like trade in bananas and regulation of smartphones, policy decisions and strategies are interwoven across national boundaries. It is increasingly hard to find any issue that is truly domestic, and every international issue increasingly hinges on international collaboration.

Some interweaving is internal to government; other interweaving involves multiple partners across sectoral and global boundaries.

Three things are clear. Interweaving has become the dominant strategy for governmental action. It is creating sharp fissures with the Progressive tradition of governmental power constrained by clear boundaries. And it is ever more challenging to manage and to hold accountable.

IMPLICATIONS OF INTERWOVEN GOVERNANCE

The late Martha Derthick, one of the shrewdest observers of American politics, explained policymakers' growing taste for such indirect policy tools. As she put it, "Congress loves action—it thrives on policy proclamation and goal setting—but it hates bureaucracy and taxes, which are the instruments of action. Overwhelmingly, it has resolved this dilemma by turning over the bulk of administration to the state governments or any organizational entity it can lay its hands on whose employees are not counted on the federal payroll."[18] It has become increasingly convenient to disconnect policymaking from its execution and to disconnect the elements of policy execution from each other. Woodrow Wilson imagined government could improve by borrowing a murderous fellow's knack for sharpening a knife cleverly. He did not imagine that government would do so by wiping its fingerprints from the knife and the other tools it uses. A more complex world and more ambitious governmental policies, of course, require more complex administrative systems. But most of government's growth has happened by remote control. It has become a distinctive pattern of administration in the United States, and it increasingly distinguishes American government from the rest of the world. And it is a fundamental result of the gradual disconnection of the philosophy of the Progressive movement from the tools and tactics to manage its programs well.

This system of government by remote control, through a network of proxies, has also created a jumbled system of accountability. Neither the president nor Congress can directly grab many of the levers of policy action. It has become harder to understand and explain what is happening because the line of sight from policy decisions to their execution has become increasingly indirect, through a web of interwoven services. That, in turn, has only increased the tendency toward "gotcha" journalism focused on government managers. If a contractor misbehaves, the only handy person into whose face to point a microphone is the federal official charged with managing the program, but that official is often light-years away from the front lines and has only indirect control of the program, at best. It is little wonder that citizens find government large, confusing, and out of control—because, too often, it is. And it is also no surprise that Americans seem so ill-informed about government and what it does, since its strategies and tactics are profoundly complex and befuddling, hard to understand and explain, let alone manage well.

Without intention or design, the result has been rising friction between the Progressives' commitment to competence, which created a plan to empower and expand government while holding it accountable, and the pragmatic steps both Republicans and Democrats took over more than a century, which wore away its basic features. Government expanded—but the protective strategies, rooted in clear boundaries to control action—eroded (see figure 4-10). It is scarcely surprising that a more complex world and more ambitious governmental policies have led to more complex administrative systems. But the erosion of the boundaries of Progressivism has created huge challenges for governmental performance, as we will see in chapter 5. It has made government more difficult to manage. It has also increased the interweaving of government into the lives of Americans, making it harder to identify just who is in charge of doing what. The elements of this system have become operated more by remote control, as the changes in the federal workforce demonstrate. As remote-control policy has grown, so too has the remarkable degree to which government has

Figure 4-10. Patterns of Progressivism

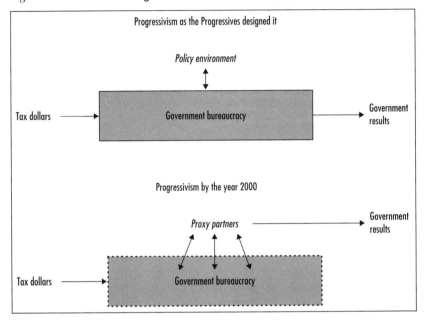

become interwoven into the lives of those who touch its policy. In ways often too subtle for most citizens—and policymakers—to understand—this interweaving has become the real face of "big government."

Perhaps most important of all, this gradual evolution of American governance has blurred the boundaries of who is responsible for what. The Progressives made their case for a growing government by promising protection from tyranny with boundaries around government's power, reinforced by a clear rule of law.[19] The growing role of proxies, however, undermined the Progressives' careful balance. Government's reach grew through advances in its tool kit, but the tool kit grew without a clear rule of law to govern the accountability of the tools. John Gaus, one of the nation's best public administration scholars during the New Deal, recognized the problem early on. As the powers of government "intermesh widely with those of industry, commerce, and finance," he warned in 1936, "the traditional restraints upon the discretion of the administrator" become inadequate.[20] The powers grew without a plan to shape, direct, and manage them.

Accountability and power, public and private became blended, with government's own rules and procedures mixing with private sector market incentives and law. The result has been a shared policy action, but there is no real constitutional accountability because the system is largely beyond the boundaries of what the authors of the Constitution envisioned. The result of this vast expansion of government by proxy is a system that has neither a clear rule of law nor a clear plan for accountability.[21] The government has created partnerships with private and nonprofit partners and pursued public policies by enlisting them—along with their own goals, incentives, and procedures—in pursuit of public policies. Both policymaking and policy execution have become shared. Policy accountability has become blended in a system that makes it increasingly hard to determine just who is in charge of what.

That is a deeply hidden but profoundly important effect of the evolution of American government in the last half of the 20th century. It is a foundation for Jurassic government—and, as we will see in chapter 5, the performance of American government.

FIVE

Risky Business

THE FIRST TRAGEDY OF SUPERSTORM Sandy's savage assault on the northeastern United States in the fall of 2012 was its vast toll— 117 lives and $60 billion in property damage, the second highest in American history after Hurricane Katrina in 2005. But the tragedy, as many residents in the hard-hit area claimed two years later, was that they had been cheated out of their flood insurance claims, even though they had paid their premiums on time and had suffered clear flood damage. *60 Minutes* reporter Sharyn Alfonsi asked Bob Kaible, a resident of Long Beach, New York, what it had been like.[1] After the storm, Kaible said, "we got back to the house and we were devastated." As he told Alfonsi, "Everything that you worked so hard in your life to get is now gone." He was up to date on his insurance payments and expected his insurer to make good on his claim, which seemed obvious to him: The storm had knocked the house off its foundation, but his insurance company planned to pay him just $79,000 of his $250,000. The reason? The insurance company said that the house was "not structurally damaged" by the storm and that, in fact, the damage that Kaible claimed was "long term," predating Sandy.

Kaible could not believe it. When he complained to his insurance company, officials sent the same engineer back for a second look. On that visit, the engineer quietly dug his original report out of his car trunk, which had found "structural damage." He showed it to Kaible, who carefully photographed the page and compared it with the report the company had shown him, which had not found storm-related damage. The same thing happened in another case, where an engineer had documented storm damage, but the official report said, "Settlement due to consolidation of soil caused the foundation wall to crack." The engineer, Andrew Braum, told Alfonsi, "That's not what I wrote. It's completely altered." Alfonsi's conclusion: Insurance companies had systematically rewritten the reports of the engineers they had hired to reduce the damage assessments—and thus to reduce the claims they would have to pay.

Alfonsi then visited FEMA Deputy Associate Administrator Brad Kieserman, who had been running the program for just three weeks. Why hadn't FEMA been more aggressive in overseeing the program, Alfonsi demanded, and why hadn't the agency moved more quickly in investigating problems like the ones that happened to Kaible and his neighbors? Alfonsi pressed Kieserman about whether he took responsibility for the behavior of insurance companies and the engineers who evaluated the damage:

> SHARYN ALFONSI: We have homeowners who went through the appeals process. And the attorneys who are being paid for by FEMA called them thieves, said they were trying to conduct fraud. Those are your dogs at the end of the leash. Do you take any responsibility for that?

BRAD KIESERMAN: Yes, I take responsibility for the fact that when FEMA funds activities, the people who are getting paid by those funds need to behave in a professional, ethical manner.

Kieserman said that individuals who thought their claims had been unfairly handled could request a review.[2] That was a huge commitment, with as many as 144,000 claims involved, including 2,200 that were in litigation. FEMA also requested that the insurance and engineering firms give residents access to the reports on the structural damage they suffered.

In both the CBS report and in citizens' eyes, the target was on FEMA's back: Why were homeowners who had dutifully paid their flood insurance premiums and suffered serious damage in Sandy having their claims denied or reduced? After all, it was a federal program. FEMA was in charge of it. So, they reasoned, FEMA should make sure that the payments were made. But the story was not nearly that simple. FEMA neither provides insurance nor manages claims. Rather, its analysts define the flood plains—the parts of the country most vulnerable to damage in case of flooding along riverbanks, oceans, and inlets. FEMA then works with local governments to help them reduce the vulnerability of their communities from floods, by encouraging local governments to write zoning and planning policies to discourage citizens from building in harm's way. FEMA built a network of more than 80 private insurance companies, who agreed to provide insurance to anyone at risk at a uniform national rate.[3] When damage occurs, the insurance companies process the claims, through the basic steps used throughout the insurance industry: They send out adjusters to assess the loss and determine how much the homeowner will receive. After big disasters, they bring in extra help, such as consulting engineers to assess property losses. That was just what happened with Sandy, as overwhelmed private insurers hired contractors to help process claims. In some cases, they then tinkered with the reports to reduce their losses. FEMA found itself at the core of the controversy, even though the problems had arisen from the behavior of private companies. Most big problems soon become governmental problems, many big governmental problems become federal ones, and everyone expects government to solve them all.

Although flood insurance is a federal program, the feds at best "manage" the program only indirectly, through private insurance companies and local governments. When residents who suffered Sandy damage complained that they were not getting the checks they thought they were entitled to, it was because of the tangled private network responsible for managing the claims process—but they blamed FEMA for the problem. FEMA, after all, has more than 4,000 employees to manage this relief program among its many other responsibilities. FEMA's flood administrator, Brad Kieserman, was the logical single person for CBS's Alfonsi to put in the crosshairs, but he had only loose control over the checks that residents thought they deserved and never received.

That mirrored the even more serious problems when Hurricane Katrina put New Orleans underwater in 2005. FEMA Administrator Michael Brown received most of the blame for the government's sluggish response. When President Bush visited the devastated area days after the storm hit, he put his arm around the administrator and said, "Brownie, you're doing a heckuva job," at a time when it was tough to claim any government official was doing a heckuva job. Ten years later, Brown was still stinging from his role as the emblem of poor management. He told *National Journal*, "We were having a very difficult time getting a unified command structure set up." The governor of Louisiana and the mayor of New Orleans opposed federalizing the response, which made it even harder to coordinate the response. Brown explained, "FEMA is really just a giant orchestra conductor with a checkbook."[4] It took a long time to get the orchestra to play together. He singled out other members of the orchestra, especially New Orleans Mayor Ray Nagin and Louisiana Governor Kathleen

Blanco, who, he believed, failed to play their notes well. Nagin was reelected as mayor. Facing a rising tide of Republicans in the state, Blanco decided not to run again and was succeeded by Republican Bobby Jindal. Brown was the only one fired.

An important implication of the growing interpenetration of policy and politics in the United States is the growing difficulty of determining who is responsible for anything, especially when more players play a role in everything. It makes it a challenge to hold anyone accountable, since everyone can—rightly—point out that they were not in charge and that others contributed potholes and roadblocks. More generally, it has created an instinct toward rising federalization: a growing expectation that the government will tackle big problems, no matter their source; an increasing instinct that tackling those problems requires a strong federal role to steer governmental programs; and an escalating need by reporters covering big stories to paint a target on someone responsible, which leads federal managers like FEMA's Brown and the flood insurance program's Kieserman to find themselves in the crosshairs, deservedly or not. When, in turn, they struggle to extract results from interwoven partners that they do not control and over whom they often have little leverage, it feeds the nagging, growing sense of government's ineffectiveness.

Relying on private partners satisfies the American instinct for small government. It makes it easier to keep government small—at least measured by the number of bureaucrats—while managing programs. It also creates more flexibility and brings in creative and innovative ideas. But no matter how much tactical and pragmatic sense the tsunami of interweaving makes, it is inevitably harder to manage and hold accountable. That, in turn, makes it risky business.

MORE PROXIES, MORE RISK

One of the best indicators of the problems that flow from this pattern is the "high-risk list" prepared by the U.S. Government Accountability

Office. Since 1990 GAO has published a biennial list of the federal programs most prone to fraud, waste, abuse, and mismanagement. It is not reading for the fainthearted—the list includes some of government's most important programs and biggest problems. Some programs have been on the list since the beginning, like defense weapons acquisition, Medicare, NASA's acquisition management, and contract management by the Department of Energy. Some are newer entries, like health care in the Department of Veterans Affairs and information technology acquisitions. The 2015 list has 32 programs in all. They are a varied lot, but there is a common element running through the list: 28 of the 32 programs work through some kind of proxy strategy (see table 5-1).

Proxy-based programs are inevitably more complex than programs the government administers directly. They involve an even-more-complex chain of management than the federal flood insurance program. More complex programs are harder to manage. Harder-to-manage programs are more likely to produce problems of performance and accountability. Programs that link players in different agencies and sectors are more difficult to coordinate. And some of these problems are extremely costly. In 2014 the federal government made $125 billion in improper payments, mostly in the Medicare, Medicaid, and Earned Income Tax Credit programs (a tax expenditure program that is part of the "enforcement of tax laws" program).[5] The $125 billion in improper payments is enough to pay for 125 years of the Smithsonian, 21 years of federal disaster relief, four years of foreign aid, and two years of medical care for veterans, and just about enough to pay the annual salary for every member of the armed forces—all from overpayments in proxy-based programs.[6]

Starving the beast—eroding government's capacity to manage programs they oppose but cannot cut—has paved the road to waste and failure. The logic is simple. If there is not enough political support for a frontal assault on reducing the size of government, conservatives for decades have argued that draining away tax revenue to support

Table 5-1. High-Risk Programs in the Federal Government

PROGRAM OR ACTIVITY	RELIANCE ON PROXIES	TOOL
1 Limiting the federal government's fiscal exposure by better managing climate change risks	x	multisector
2 Management of federal oil and gas resources	x	regulations
3 Modernizing the U.S. financial regulatory system and the federal role in housing finance	x	regulations
4 Restructuring the U.S. Postal Service to achieve sustainable financial viability		direct
5 Funding the nation's surface transportation system	x	grants
6 Strategic human capital management	x	support
7 Managing federal real property	x	contracts
8 Improving the management of IT acquisitions and operations	x	contracts
9 Department of Defense (DOD) approach to business transformation	x	contracts
10 DOD business systems modernization	x	contracts
11 DOD support infrastructure management		support
12 DOD financial management		support
13 DOD supply chain management	x	contracts
14 DOD weapon systems acquisition	x	contracts
15 Mitigating gaps in weather satellite data	x	contracts
16 Strengthening Department of Homeland Security management functions	x	support and contracts
17 Establishing effective mechanisms for sharing and managing terrorism-related information to protect the homeland	x	multisector

(*continued*)

Table 5-1. (*continued*)

PROGRAM OR ACTIVITY	RELIANCE ON PROXIES	TOOL
18 Ensuring the security of federal information systems and cyber critical infrastructure and protecting the privacy of personally identifiable information	x	multisector
19 Ensuring the effective protection of technologies critical to U.S. national security interests	x	multisector
20 Improving federal oversight of food safety	x	regulations
21 Protecting public health through enhanced oversight of medical products	x	regulations
22 Transforming EPA's processes for assessing and controlling toxic chemicals	x	regulations
23 DOD contract management	x	contracts
24 Department of Energy's contract management for the National Nuclear Security Administration and Office of Environmental Management	x	contracts
25 NASA acquisition management	x	contracts
26 Enforcement of tax laws	x	tax expenditures
27 Managing risks and improving Department of Veterans Affairs health care	x	direct and contracts
28 Improving and modernizing federal disability programs		direct, multiagency
29 Pension Benefit Guaranty Corporation insurance programs	x	regulations
30 Medicare program	x	contracts
31 Medicaid program	x	contracts and grants
32 National Flood Insurance Program	x	insurance and contracts

Source: U.S. Government Accountability Office, *High-Risk Series* (2015) (www.gao.gov /products/GAO-15-290), with the author's analysis.

government programs would be the next best option. Ronald Reagan boosted the strategy with his 1981 call for a tax cut. "Well, you know, we can lecture our children about extravagance until we run out of voice and breath. Or we can cure their extravagance by simply reducing their allowance," Reagan said. Bureaucrats, the logic went, cannot fuel big government if they do not have money to spend. It is no surprise that public opinion polls have shown that Republicans have a far less favorable view of federal workers (with 46 percent "favorable") than Independents (60 percent) or Democrats (79 percent).[7]

Writing in *Forbes*, conservative analyst Bruce Bartlett concluded that this starve-the-beast strategy not only failed to rein in government's growth but ended up "raising spending and making deficits worse. In short, STB [starve the beast] is a completely bankrupt notion that belongs in the museum of discredited ideas, along with things like alchemy."[8] Bartlett's argument has not convinced his conservative colleagues, who continue to fight to cripple programs they cannot kill. In 2013 the *National Review* argued for defunding Obama's Affordable Care Act instead of trying to repeal it.[9] Then in 2014, when the Department of Veterans Affairs stumbled into a series of problems in providing care to vets, Republicans pushed through legislation to make it easier to fire poor-performing bureaucrats—and pressed new VA Secretary Robert A. McDonald to fire more feds and to fire them faster.

It is easy to understand Republicans' frustration in failing to bend the bureaucracy to their will. Government spending has continued to grow—not just for Obama's Affordable Care Act but for other expensive ventures, such as the wars in Iraq and Afghanistan and an ever-rising collection of tax breaks. They were irritated by the increasing reach and scope of government and were committed to using any tool they could find to stop its growing influence. That, however, also hindered government's ability to do the things, including those we explored in chapter 1, that just about everyone agrees government must do.

Of course, the Democrats have often been no better in building a government that works. It would be hard to imagine a bigger embarrassment to Barack Obama than the collapse of the website supporting the launch of Obamacare, Healthcare.gov, in October 2013. The failure to plan the website carefully caused the cost for the health exchanges to balloon from $56 million to $209 million, and the cost for the data hub increased from $30 million to $80 million. The agency managing the launch, the Centers for Medicare and Medicaid Services (CMS), exercised such poor oversight that its staff gave the green light 40 times to contractors for work, even though it had not been properly examined in advance. Most important, GAO found in its investigation, "CMS launched Healthcare.gov without verification that it met performance requirements"—that is, the feds went live with the website without checking to see if it would work.[10]

These problems, however, did not flow from a starved beast. The wounds, instead, were largely self-inflicted. In the Obama administration's single most important initiative, everyone in the administration wanted it to work. The problems flowed from managers who did not have their eyes on the ball—and who too often did not have the capacity to get the job done. Desperate to put the program back on track after its catastrophic launch, Obama deputized his former OMB deputy director for management, Jeff Zients, to get it straightened out. Zients built a small but muscular team of government officials and private experts, who worked punishing hours. Within three months, the site was working far more reliably. Poor management helped create the problem; great management quickly helped solve it. It had been a solvable problem. The administration simply had failed to recognize just how important management of the program was to begin with.

The Obamacare story is a premier case of the problems that over time rose to cripple the bipartisan Progressive consensus on competence: efforts by some partisans to kneecap a program they could not kill, and the failure of other partisans to nurture a program they desperately wanted to work. By two different roads, the two sides ended up at the same place, with a program passed by Congress and signed by the president that stumbled at its launch. Citizens, in the end, concluded yet again that government simply could not get its act together.

Debating *what* government should do surely has a legitimate place at the policy table. It is an absolutely crucial element of any democracy, has long been at the core of governance in America, and stood at the center of the traditional, bipartisan Progressive consensus. There were constant battles between conservatives and liberals about just what government should do. But once those battles were decided, no matter how uneasily, there was consensus that government owed its citizens a competent government that executed the decisions that policymakers reached. That consensus about the *how* of government, however, gradually evaporated in the last third of the 20th century and completely broke down in the partisan wrangling of the early 2000s.

The evidence from GAO's careful analysis is clear: Getting good performance from government, even in the most complex interwoven programs, is hard but possible. Doing hard things well requires building government's capacity. Trying to cut it by starving it can often drive costs up and confidence down, without really changing its size much at all.

PROBLEMS FROM THE TAP

Making cuts in the wrong places can do real harm, as residents in West Virginia's Elk River Valley found in 2014. On a chilly January morning, they turned on their taps to discover a strong smell of black licorice in their drinking water. Some residents came to local hospitals with nausea, vomiting, and eye infections. Government officials scrambled to truck in drinking water. Schools and restaurants closed, and hospitals limited surgeries. The state's Department of Environmental Protection suspected problems at a Freedom

Industries chemical plant and sent inspectors out to check. "No, we're not having any problems," company officials said. "What are you talking about?" But the state inspectors found a pool of chemicals that had leaked out of a hole in one of the company's storage tanks. It was tricky to tell at first where it was going, because the nearby Elk River was frozen over, but inspectors soon concluded that the chemicals were disappearing under the ice into the river, a short distance upstream from the state's largest drinking-water intake.[11]

Freedom Industries had a government permit for the property and its tanks. The permit required them to promptly report any spills, but the state's Department of Environmental Protection said that they had not received any report. The delay in discovering the problem compounded the crisis, because it made containing and then cleaning up the spill far worse. The chemical turned out to be 4-methylcyclohexane methanol (MCHM), used in coal-fired power plants, and it was nasty-smelling stuff. But just how dangerous was it? Government investigators had a tough time answering that question. The manufacturer of the chemical provided the information sheet required by the federal Occupational Safety and Health Administration but, as Ken Ward, a prize-winning reporter for the *Charleston Gazette* reporter discovered, the information was sparse. "Is it a carcinogen? No data. Does it cause developmental problems? No data." That left both government officials and local citizens on their own to figure out what to do. Ward made his own decision, he said. "My family and I, we're not drinking this water."[12] But the government's toxic chemical inventory just did not contain enough information to provide guidance to residents about just how much danger they were in.

What could be done to prevent these problems? In a radio interview, Ward explained that industry officials "insisted there's enough regulation already and that agencies like the Environmental Protection Agency and the Occupational Safety and Health Administration do enough already." Then he added:

I think there seems to be this idea that . . . agencies like EPA and OSHA are these jackbooted thugs that are kicking down the gates of manufacturing facilities and stomping out jobs. When in fact, a lot of these facilities will go for years and years without ever seeing an OSHA inspector coming in and checking on the workplace conditions; without ever seeing an EPA inspector who is looking at their environmental conditions. The notion that these places are just terribly overregulated is wildly exaggerated.[13]

It is impossible to provide citizens with adequate inspection of their drinking water if there are not enough inspectors.

No one wants to take a chance of getting sick from drinking water out of the tap. Government has regulations to prevent that from happening; a different EPA program is charged with creating a government database on the risks different chemicals pose. In this case, the inspection teams were not large enough to examine the plant, and there was not enough information on the toxic chemicals inventory to assess the risk from the spill. Federal and state government officials knew the spill was nasty, they suspected it was dangerous, but they did not know just how dangerous. In fact, two weeks later the company revealed that a second chemical, a concoction of polyglycol ethers called PPH, had also been part of the brew. That only compounded the investigation—and the worries. Even after the local water company lifted its "do not use" order, the federal Centers for Disease Control recommended that pregnant women continue to avoid it. A committee of the West Virginia state senate heard from the federal Chemical Safety Board that no amount of any of the chemicals was acceptable in drinking water.[14]

Local residents did not need that warning—the smell of licorice and the feelings of nausea had been enough to convince most residents. Not every toxic chemical leaves such telltale signs. The system responsible for ensuring safe drinking water, however, is complex, with private industry as the first defense and with government inspectors—federal, state, and local—working to ensure that industry meets the regulatory standards. We do not always know which chemicals are dangerous, at what level they can cause harm, and how much government inspection of private industry is enough to safeguard the public. No one wants an overbearing government, but everyone wants a government strong enough to prevent danger from the tap.

BAD MANAGEMENT IS BAD POLITICS

In yet another *60 Minutes* story, first broadcast in September 2014, reporter Steve Kroft looked into the growing problem of fraudsters who file bogus tax returns, using stolen identities, to collect refunds. Such scams are estimated to cost the Treasury at least $5.2 billion a year. Kroft told his viewers, "You'd think the IRS would have come up with a way to stop it, [but] it hasn't." He added, "Proving once again, what every con man already knows: There is no underestimating the general dysfunction and incompetence of government bureaucracy."[15]

The problem—both government's performance and the widespread cynicism about its ability to produce results—is huge and getting bigger. But is Kroft's reporting truly a case of "the general dysfunction and incompetence of government bureaucracy"? The first point, of course, is that it is not bureaucratic incompetence that leads individuals to steal taxpayers' identities and then steal tax refunds. That is a problem generated by criminals with larceny in their hearts. Why hasn't the IRS stopped it? In fact, it is possible to block fraudulent payments by checking an individual's identity before sending a refund, but it is hard to do that *and* mail refunds promptly. Employers are required to deliver paper copies of the W-2 to taxpayers by February 1 each year. The electronic versions of the W-2 are not required to be delivered to the IRS until March 31. Employers with fewer than 25 workers do not have to file the forms electronically at all.[16]

So the IRS could wait to mail out refunds until it has completed the matching process, which could take until May or later—or it could mail out the refunds as the returns are received and follow up later with the computerized matches. Faced with the dilemma of creating millions of unhappy taxpayers waiting many months for their refunds or taking the risk of some fraudulent refunds being sent—and then trying to track them down later—the IRS leaned toward making fewer taxpayers (and their elected members of Congress) even more unhappy. There are two other options: requiring employers to submit their electronic W-2 files much earlier; and requiring smaller employers, perhaps with more than five instead of 25 employees, to send in electronic W-2 files as well. Both steps, however, would be more expensive for employers, both would first require congressional action, and employers would be sure to resist new government regulations that would prove more costly for them.

This is not an example of "the general dysfunction and incompetence of government bureaucracy." The IRS was caught between clever criminals who had discovered a new way to bilk the government, tough policy trade-offs, and an inability to shift course without congressional approval. Of course, the story is too complicated for media coverage, and blaming tax collectors is a time-proven tool for stirring the public's attention. That has worked since biblical days.

Major management problems inevitably become political problems. Elected officials naturally want to deflect blame. Reporters need to find an easy handhold on complicated issues. Citizens want their government programs to work, do not want to pay high taxes, and do not like anything restraining their liberty. (Of course, there is nothing new here—that is a description of the American colonies in 1776, too.) So management in general and bureaucrats in particular become the lightning rods for dysfunction in American political life. Sometimes, as with many of GAO's high-risk areas, the blame is deserved.

Sometimes, as in the case of the IRS's struggles with identity fraud, it is not. Either way, this challenge feeds into the broader narrative that each of the political parties has developed: Democrats often pay far more attention to policy decisions than they do to figuring out how to make them work, and Republicans often disinvest in management as a way of stopping policies they do not like. Coupled with the increasing complexity of American government management because of the rise of proxies, the Progressives' commitment to competence has fallen on profoundly hard times, not only in delivering public services but in building the foundation for trust in government's ability to deliver.

There is little political payoff in successful program execution. No one has even seen a headline proclaiming, "Mail Delivered Yet Again Today" or "Thousands of Planes Land Safely at Destination Airports." Citizens rightly expect value for their tax dollars, and they are not likely to applaud a government that does what they pay it to do. But the political costs for administrative failures can be huge and lasting, and such failures sneak up on presidents when they least expect it. As tougher problems and proxy administration make government more complex, the political risks from management failures are growing.

Two of the biggest administrative crises in the 2000s were deeply interwoven into the government's proxy strategy: the struggle to recover from Katrina's devastation in 2005 and the Obama administration's failure to launch its Healthcare.gov website in 2013. In both cases, the political damage was enormous. In the Bush administration, the point at which the president's negatives exceeded his positives and never recovered was in the aftermath of Katrina (figure 5-1). At almost precisely the same point in his presidency, Obama suffered a serious blow to his popularity because of the troubled website launch, and he struggled to recover afterward (figure 5-2). Presidents often pay little attention to management issues, until management failures impose enormous political costs, often when they least expect it. Management failures are bad politics. Avoiding them requires paying

Figure 5-1. Bush Approval Rating

Percent

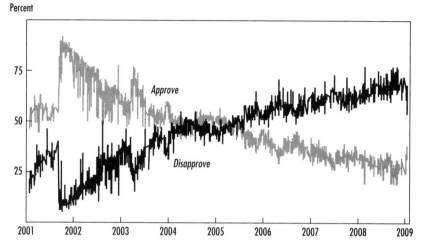

Source: Roper Center (www.ropercenter.uconn.edu/polls/presidential-approval/).

Figure 5-2. Obama Approval Rating

Percent

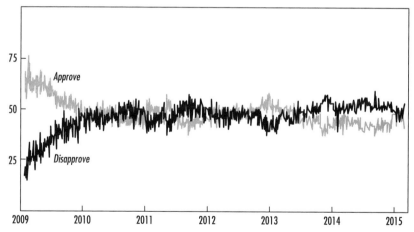

Source: Roper Center (www.ropercenter.uconn.edu/polls/presidential-approval/).

careful attention. And it requires a keen eye for building the capacity government needs to manage well.

It is possible to improve the results even from the most troubled programs, as GAO's high-risk analysis has shown. But it is also inevitable that poorly managed programs will cause political fallout. If there is little upside from good management, there can be catastrophic implications from bad management. Government's growing reliance on complex proxy tools makes it harder to manage well—and, therefore, makes big political problems more likely. Interweaving is a good thing. It makes it easier to marshal the expertise needed to make government work without building a big government to do the work. It is a more complicated thing than direct government management, and, as interweaving becomes more complex and intricate, it strays farther from the Progressives' commitment to competence—and farther from government's capacity to ensure that programs are managed well. The biggest problems flow from trying to use an outmoded strategy, based in the Progressives, to manage policy strategies that no longer fit the Progressive model championed by Republicans and Democrats alike. It is increasingly clear that bad management is bad politics.

THE SLIDE IN TRUST OF GOVERNMENT

This has all happened amid declining trust in governmental institutions. It is too much of a reach to suggest that the rise of indirect, proxy government is directly responsible for the decline in public trust—but it certainly has not helped.

In 1964, 77 percent of Americans trusted the government just about always or most of the time. Since then, the trend has been downward. After the September 11 terrorist attacks, trust recovered from the post-Watergate malaise, to about 50 percent. But it tumbled afterward, to an unsteady plateau of about 20 percent in 2010 (see figure 5-3). This fundamental distrust has spilled over to Americans'

Figure 5-3. Trust in Government

Percent of respondents

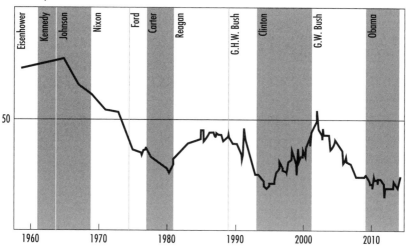

Source: Trust in government "just about always" or "most of the time." Pew Research Center (www.people-press.org/2014/11/13/public-trust-in-government/).

views of which group—big business, big labor, or big government—poses the biggest threat. Since the 1960s, big government has led, and concern has steadily grown. In 1965, 35 percent of those responding said the biggest threat was big government. By 2013 the number had more than doubled, to 72 percent.[17] A 2014 Rasmussen poll found that 37 percent of likely voters feared the federal government, and 54 percent of respondents believe that the federal government is a threat to individual liberty, rather than a protector. Two-thirds of respondents saw the federal government as "a special interest group that looks out primarily for its own interests," a profound worry for a government whose job is to look out for its people.[18] The share of Americans who said they were "angry" at the federal government grew from 11 percent in 1997 to 30 percent in 2013.[19]

There is evidence, however, that the closer government's connection with the people, the more the people trust it. Compared with the federal government, trust in state and local governments has remained

Figure 5-4. Americans' Trust in State and Local Government

Percent

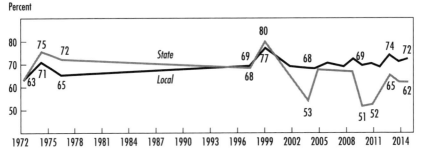

Source: Gallup, "Americans Still Trust Local Government More Than State," September 22, 2014 (www.gallup.com/poll/176846/americans-trust-local-government-state.aspx).
Note: Figures are percentages with a great deal/fair amount of trust in the level of government.

far higher and much more stable. As figure 5-4 shows, trust in local government was little changed in the generation from 1972 through 2014. Trust in state government has remained relatively steady, except for several rocky patches in the 2000s when states struggled to pass their budgets. International comparisons reinforce this conclusion. The OECD found that citizens' satisfaction with government services was higher for programs that provided benefits (like health care and education) and for those with whom they had more direct contact (like local police). The closer citizens' contact with government, the higher their satisfaction, although the OECD also found that higher satisfaction with services did not mean greater trust in government. Still, citizens showed they could distinguish between different services, based on how they connected with them.[20] "Trust tends to be highest at the local level," the OECD found, where services are delivered and where the link with government performance is most concrete. Trust also tends to be higher for actual users of public services than for nonusers. Public confidence in public services tended to be highest in local police, health care, and education, which in most countries involved a direct relationship between government service providers and citizens.[21]

Overall, there seems to be a pattern: The looser the connection between citizens and those who serve them, the more difficult it is to build trust in that relationship. On the other hand, good government performance does not necessarily seem to increase trust. Moreover, governments have been able to govern, in the United States and abroad, without necessarily having high levels of trust from their citizens.[22] The scholar Russell Hardin suggests that declining public trust in government might be the product of "intolerance of ambiguity," as problems get harder and strategies to solve them become more complex.[23] And the more ambiguous each of the elements of government becomes, the more trust in government suffers.

It is hard to be sure, but the transformation from the Progressive model, with strong government agencies working within tight boundaries, to complex interweaving might well be playing an important role in diminishing the trust of citizens in government. It creates complicated programs that are increasingly challenging to manage. It disconnects citizens from the governmental apparatus that serves them and makes it tough for them—and, for that matter, for policymakers and journalists—to determine just who is responsible for what. In short, it decreases the "line of sight" from citizens to the government that serves them and the elected officials who govern them. That, in turn, has escalated everyone's expectations about what government can and should do, since if no one is fully responsible for anything, anyone can be responsible for everything. It makes it easier for private citizens and private companies to duck their own responsibilities, call on "government" (whatever that is) to step in when they need help, expect that somehow the vastly interwoven system will deliver, and complain when problems occur, as they inevitably do in complex and messy programs pursuing ambitious goals without enough capacity to ensure success.

To tackle this problem, and especially to connect the many threads of the interwoven policy scheme, government needs new tools. One of the most promising is greater reliance on information and evidence, and we turn to that strategy in chapter 6.

SIX

Evidence

SHERLOCK HOLMES POINTED OUT TO Dr. Watson in *The Adventure of the Speckled Band* "how dangerous it always is to reason from insufficient data." In the 21st-century information age, that counsel is even more important, because it is sensible—indeed, essential—to conclude that better government requires better information, and that better information hinges on much more sophisticated evidence.

In the 2014 book *Moneyball for Government*, former OMB directors Jim Nussle and Peter Orszag point to the revolutionary success of the Oakland Athletics in using evidence to play better baseball. The A's developed a strategy called "Moneyball" to drive the team's most important decisions, and they used it in 2002 to amazing success. Why can't government do the same thing, Nussle and Orszag wondered? But, they reported sadly, their own estimates suggested that "less than one dollar out of every hundred dollars the federal government spends is backed by even the most basic evidence." Moneyball for government—more use of better evidence—could vastly improve government's results, they argued.[1]

In fact, we have evidence—of some kind—for *all* the governmental decisions we make. The problem is that some of it might not be valid. Some is not very persuasive. And some of it is just plain wrong. If we are going to have better government, we need better evidence, to supplement the better bureaucrats I argued for in chapter 3. Just as is the case in the private sector, governments surely will be swamped with more information and evidence, from all sources. For government, the trick will be harnessing better evidence and using it drive better policy results. Coupled with better bureaucrats, that is the foundation for recovering government's competence. Just how well we do that will determine how effectively we can close the gap between the Progressive philosophy and the interwoven, hard-to-manage programs it created.

FIGURING OUT WHAT WE KNOW

Consider seven propositions about how what we know—and what we think we know—shape the making and execution of government policy.

There is knowledge—of some kind—behind everything we do

Decision makers never decide in a vacuum and, at least most of the time, they do their best to know what they are doing. There is always evidence of some kind, even if it is a feeling in the pit of a decision maker's stomach, behind every decision. But it is also likely that much of the evidence used to make decisions is not very good. As Charles E. Lindblom and David K. Cohen wrote in a lively little book back in 1979, analysts often "greatly underestimate the society's use—and necessary use—of an existing stock" of knowledge. In fact, what they call "ordinary knowledge" is everywhere, flowing from "common sense, casual empiricism, or thoughtful speculation and analysis."[2] Everyone has knowledge at their disposal, and that is what they use in making judgments and decisions. The problem is that some of this knowledge is not thorough, proven, or effective in illuminating good answers to important questions—or even in making sure we are asking the right questions.

Some of what we think we know has not been investigated carefully or rigorously tested—and some of it is just plain wrong

A 2013 public opinion poll found that 21 percent of voters think that a UFO crashed in Roswell, New Mexico, in 1947; 29 percent think aliens exist; 20 percent of voters believe there is a link between childhood vaccines and autism; 7 percent believe that the moon landing was a fake; and 4 percent believe that lizard people gain political power and control society.[3] The Animal Planet television network made a huge success of the show *Finding Bigfoot*, including the revelation that "New Jersey is a Sasquatch playground."[4] (In a survey, 14 percent of respondents said they think Bigfoot exists.) However, *Finding Bigfoot* has never found a Sasquatch, and the Roswell alien is elusive (although some believe that is because the alien has been moved to Wright Patterson Air Force Base in Ohio). The evidence is pretty persuasive Americans walked on the moon, no one has seen lizard people, and careful research has found no link between vaccines and autism.

Moreover, everyone knows that a fire department needs to speed to a fire to save lives. However, evidence shows that speeding can risk the lives of firefighters and others on the roadway. In fact, the International Association of Fire Chiefs has found that vehicle crashes were the second leading cause of firefighter fatalities. "You can't help," one of the association's handouts noted, "if you don't arrive."[5] Texas allows emergency vehicles to exceed the speed limit, as long as they do not endanger lives or property, but it is hard to know where the line is until it is crossed and an accident occurs. That has led other departments to limit the speed of emergency apparatus to no more than 10 miles per hour over the posted speed limit. Getting better answers for the things we think we already know can be very challenging.

We know something about everything, but we do not know
everything with the same confidence—and we do not
always know how much we need to know before we act

In May 2011 President Obama approved a special mission by the Navy's Seal Team 6 to attack a hideout in Abbottabad, Pakistan. It was an extremely risky mission aimed at taking out Osama bin Laden, who had directed the September 11 terrorist attacks. Before launching the mission, the president did not know for certain whether bin Laden was in the hideout. Nor could he be sure about how much uncertainty was too much on which to risk the lives of the Seal Team or the political embarrassment of failure. After the mission, Defense Secretary Leon Panetta told *Time* magazine that his aides were 60–80 percent confident that bin Laden was hiding in the compound.[6] The CIA's lead intelligence analyst put the number at 90–95 percent. The deputy director of the CIA estimated the chances at 60 percent. The CIA had created a "red team" to do the worst-case analysis, and the team estimated that there was just a 30–40 percent chance that bin Laden was at Abbottabad. President Obama concluded that the chances were between 45 and 55 percent, according to an interview later with *60 Minutes* on CBS television.[7]

Then, after Seal Team 6 successfully stormed the compound, there was the challenge of making sure that the body was bin Laden's, especially since he had not been reliably sighted in years. The Defense Intelligence Agency had moved a special laboratory to Afghanistan and, within eight hours, completed a DNA match that confirmed bin Laden had been killed.[8] Obama had to make a black-or-white decision about whether to commit American troops. Then he had to make a public announcement about bin Laden's death, all in a world where nothing was certain and where the costs of being wrong were enormous. In both cases, the evidence proved the raid a good call, but every step along the way was bathed in uncertainty.

We increasingly know more about more things

In 2009 Britain's *Guardian* newspaper said that information on the Internet had reached 500 billion gigabytes, enough to fill two iPods (of the day) for every person on Earth. If printed in books, the stack would stretch from Earth to Pluto ten times.[9] The pace of technological change is likely to accelerate the flood of information. In 2010 Google CEO Eric Schmidt argued that humans create as much information every two days as they did from the dawn of civilization through 2003. As Schmidt said, "I spend most of my time assuming the world is not ready for the technology revolution that will be happening to them soon."[10] In 2013 *Science Daily* argued that 90 percent of all the data in the world had been produced in the previous two years.[11] Much of this information, like Facebook posts, is short and fleeting, but all of it adds immensely to the volume of information. By the time the cursor on my computer reaches the end of this sentence, all those numbers will be dated; by the time you read this, the numbers will be obsolete. Humans are producing information at an accelerating pace, and there is a growing gap between the information produced and the information that anyone can—or would—want to use. Policymakers are drowning in information.

We do not know enough about many important things

Some problems are studied much more than others. Academic journals have attracted a great deal of careful research on strategies for reducing poverty and crime, in part because these areas generate large data sets and fit the methods of careful statistical analysis and controlled experimentation that academic researchers aggressively pursue. But not everything gets the same attention. In its 2015 plan for strengthening the federal workforce, the Office of Management and Budget identified areas where there was the biggest gap between the skills the government most needed and the skills it had in its workforce: information and cybersecurity policy, acquisitions, economics, human resources, auditing, and the connection between STEM (science, technology, engineering, and math) and policy.[12] These are areas of intense government work where the supply of human capital lags behind the demand—and where the government, as a result, does not know what it needs to know. There is an old joke about the drunk who looks for lost keys under a lamppost because that is where the light is. In many cases, government needs answers to some problems that do not sit underneath the lamp, and it does not have a good flashlight to find them.

What we think we know is shaped by our interaction with others

We often do not decide what we know from self-reflection and individual study. Knowing is a social process, shaped by our interactions with others, especially with those we tend to agree with. Cutting-edge work by authors like Irving L. Janis, Cass Sunstein, and Reid Hastie point to the dangers of "groupthink," where social interactions can amplify efforts in judgment and lead to polarizing positions.[13] Groupthink can harden evidence into a shared vision of what everyone, of course, knows (at least, according to the group) and blind members of the group to what they need to know but do not.

Sunstein tells a story of his time running the Office of Information and Regulatory Affairs in Obama's OMB. He received an anxious late-night e-mail from Nancy-Ann DeParle, who was then the president's deputy chief of staff for policy. "How's the regulation coming?" she wrote. Since he did not know which regulation she was referring to, Sunstein cheerily wrote back, "I don't know which regulation you have in mind, but most of them are coming pretty well, so chances are that this one is coming well too." DeParle's quick reply was "hug," and Sunstein, deeply touched, wrote, "That's the nicest email of the year." DeParle shot back that she was referring to "ghg," short for "greenhouse gas," and that her phone had auto-corrected the abbreviation.[14] The "ghg" regulation was in the middle of fierce debate. Both DeParle and Sunstein caught themselves—but often leaders do not. It is easy not to ask hard questions about what could go wrong, only to discover weeks or months later that the failure to dig traps them in problems they never saw coming.

Leaders use what they can usefully use and ignore what is not useful

Knowing is a political act. All information that bears on decisions has political content, because it inevitably reflects values: what was important enough to gather and keep, what sense to make of it, and what to do about it. For decision makers, the key is knowing: *gathering information good enough on which to take action*. But that frames another question: How much is *good enough?* And on that question there is a long and rich debate in policy analysis. Scholars like Charles E. Lindblom, James G. March, and Herbert A. Simon argued that decision makers could—and should—"muddle through" in making decisions, by "satisficing" (focusing on just a few major alternatives and stopping the search for new information when they find a satisfactory solution, even if more searching might produce a better one).[15] But not everyone agreed. Economist Alice Rivlin spoke for a legion of economists in writing that decision makers need "to have faith in rationality to believe that analysis of a problem generally leads to better decisions," and that "hardly anyone explicitly favors a return to muddling through."[16] For decision makers, figuring out what the evidence means—and how to act on it—is central to the process of knowing. That, in turn, is key to making and executing good decisions, a challenge ever greater as the complexity of problems increases and the volume of information multiplies.

BALANCING SUPPLY AND DEMAND

In the flood of information and evidence, several propositions are clear. There is more information, and government would be better if it used more of it, more effectively. Moreover, the *supply* of information is exploding. So too is the *demand* for information. But there is an underlying chorus of grumbles that makes matching supply and demand difficult. Those on the supply side—the policy analysts inside government and the scholars outside, all of whom produce the information and evidence—complain that decision makers do not listen. Those on the demand side—decision makers who shape policy—complain that they do not hear what they need. Analysts and academics, they say, too often produce information that arrives too late for key decisions, that is unintelligible to busy policymakers, or that provides answers that do not match the questions on the table. An imbalance of these supply and demand forces often greatly complicates the improved use of evidence in government.[17]

In some cases, however, supply and demand forces have come into remarkable balance, with dramatic results. Nothing demonstrates this more than the effort to identify the victims of the World Trade Center terrorist attack on September 11.

In the first days after the September 11 attack, rescue teams hoped that they would find survivors in the debris. Firefighters and heavy machinery operators gently sifted through the wreckage and highly trained dogs sniffed the rubble, but a sad truth soon settled over the site: There were precious few survivors to save. The rescuers soon shifted to finding and identifying those lost—343 firefighters and paramedics, 60 police officers, a member of the U.S. Secret Service, and office workers trapped as the towers collapsed. In all, 2,752 people died at the World Trade Center, and the recovery teams committed to identifying as many victims as possible to bring a measure of peace to their families.

The word *identify*, however, vastly oversimplified the problem. Debris from two 110-story buildings, as well as buildings from the rest of the complex, covered more than 16 acres. Some of the debris fell blocks away, and some of the human remains inevitably became mixed with the vast amounts of building debris trucked to Staten Island's Fresh Kill landfill, where it was scoured for bits that investigators could identify. In the decade after the attack, recovery workers found 22,000 human remains at the World Trade Center site, in the surrounding neighborhood, and at Fresh Kill.

DNA identification was in its relatively early days, and the World Trade Center identifications presented unspeakable challenges. In addition to the sheer destructive force of the collapse, which left few recognizable traces of the desks, chairs, and other office equipment in the buildings, temperatures inside the buildings had reached more than 1,800 degrees Fahrenheit before the collapse. Fires continued to burn in "the pile," as the site become known, for more than 100 days, sometimes at temperatures of 2,800 degrees.[18] Workers at the pile reported seeing molten metal dripping from mangled steel beams. To extinguish the super-hot fires, firefighters poured massive amounts of water onto the pile for weeks. That horrific brew made it clear that identifying the victims would require new DNA techniques and procedures.

Bob Shaler headed New York City's Department of Forensic Biology in the medical examiner's office, and he faced a challenge that no medical examiner had previously confronted. No identification team had ever before tried to identify so many victims of a mass casualty from DNA, let alone from so many remains that had been so badly damaged. Shaler and his colleagues quickly focused on a complex multi-organizational team. Promega, a Madison, Wisconsin, company, created a robotic DNA extraction system. Applied Biosystems built a new system for creating DNA profiles. The New York State Police collected DNA samples from the family members of victims, including painstaking work with combs and toothbrushes, and they sent DNA extracts to Myriad Genetics in Salt Lake City for analysis. Bode Technology, a Virginia-based DNA start-up company, did bone typing and, since most of the remains from the pile turned out to be bone fragments, that work proved especially important.

In the first days after the attacks, Shaler and his team thought they would be able to handle the identifications, but, within a few days, it became clear that the task lay far beyond anything that the medical examiner's office had done before. He reached out to Bode Technology's founder, Tom Bode, and said simply, "We need help."[19]

Bode Technology was an ideal partner for the medical examiner's office. Three years before, the company had assisted in identifying the "unknown soldier" from the Vietnam War who was buried in 1984 at Arlington National Cemetery. At the time, the pilot, who had been shot down in 1972, was known only as Soldier X-26 and could not be identified with the military's existing methods. The mother of Lt. Michael J. Blassie, however, heard reports that Soldier X-26 might be her son. The family convinced the Pentagon to exhume the remains and, thanks to advanced new DNA techniques, Bode Technology worked with the U.S. Armed Forces DNA Identification Lab to confirm that X-26 was in fact Lt. Blassie. His remains were returned to the family for burial with full military honors near his Missouri hometown.

Bode Technology had also helped crack cold cases in Virginia. In 1997 the company partnered with the Commonwealth of Virginia on a three-year project to perform DNA typing on 60,000 samples per year from unsolved crime investigations. The project checked DNA from crime scenes against DNA samples from felons already behind bars—and made 3,600 matches.[20] The work led to another tough project, identifying victims from the crash of Alaska Airlines Flight 261 in January 2000. A maintenance failure in the plane's tail caused the flight crew to lose control and it plummeted into the water off Los Angeles. The local coroner was able to identify about two-thirds of the victims, but the other remains required DNA analysis. The military's DNA lab was swamped with work at the time, so the identification team turned to Bode Technology, which went to work on the 860 remains recovered from the 88 victims. In three months, the company completed the identification job. At the time, it was an unimaginable feat—so many remains, so badly damaged but so carefully matched, in such a short time.[21] At each point, the company developed new techniques to solve new problems—from a single soldier to a computer match of cold cases against living suspects to extracting DNA from human remains on a far larger scale than had ever been tried before. Demand from decision makers led to vast improvements in the supply of techniques and new partnerships between private labs like Bode and government agencies.

A month after the terrorist attacks, Bode Technology sent a driver to New York to pick up the first collection of bone fragments, 2,132 in all. How quickly could the company identify the remains, Shaler asked? Bode promised that his labs would analyze 1,000 bones a week. It was a bold pledge, because neither Bode Technology nor any other lab had ever reached a rate anything like that. New processing techniques devised on the run helped the lab hit the target.

The deeper the team got into the work, however, the harder it got. Later identifications required assessment of bone fragments that often were smaller and more heavily damaged by the collapse, the intense heat, and submersion in water for weeks as the recovery work progressed. The Bode team responded by inventing a new technique called BodePlex, a fresh way of extracting DNA from samples that previously would have been unusable. The Bode lab also developed new methods for extracting mitochondrial DNA, which each of us inherits from our mothers. The work proved pathbreaking in producing even more identifications down the road.

By April 30, 2004, the team had identified 1,552 of those missing, with 812 identifications from DNA. In all, the scientists were able to identify 8,448 remains, or 64 percent of the total.[22] On May 10, 2014, three vehicles representing those lost—one from the New York City police, one a New York City fire truck, a third from the Port Authority Police Emergency Service Unit—solemnly conveyed 7,930 remains that could not be identified to the 9/11 Memorial, on the site where the twin towers fell, in the hope of future scientific advances.[23] Compared with the enormous uncertainty that Shaler and his partners faced in the early days of the effort, the identification of nearly two-thirds of the victims is miraculous.

It was a notable time in history, a remarkable concentration of scientific advances, and a reinforcement of the basic notion: Demand for better decisions, in this case, making more identifications with greater certainty, generated an increased supply of evidence, which in this case brought sophisticated new DNA applications. The identifications proved remarkably successful because the crisis spurred a fresh balance of supply and demand forces, which helped manage the crisis and brought a measure of peace to families who had suffered so much through the terrorist attacks.

THE PUZZLE OF KNOWING

The identification of the World Trade Center victims was a triumph of developing new kinds of evidence and analysis for public problems. It was also a remarkable success of interweaving the public responsibilities (of the New York medical examiner's office) with private support (especially from Bode Technology). But it also underlines a fundamental challenge. The medical examiner's office wanted to know the identities of as many of the remains as possible, but just what do we mean to talk about *knowing*? And how do we come to know enough to act? For example, what did the medical examiner's office need to know before being confident it was turning over the right remains to the right families? In the World Trade Center case, there were rare but tragic mistakes, like the case of a Long Island widow who had received the wrong remains because of a mix-up in police records and another case in which the family of a firefighter received the remains of a colleague from the same station who died with him.[24] DNA analysis resolved the cases. But they both illustrate the puzzle of gathering information good enough on which to take action. The challenge is managing the inevitable uncertainty: determining how much we know, how sure we are about knowing it, and how certain we need to be to make a decision.

Consider the case of Russian Tsar Nicholas II and his family. Historians have concluded that they were shot toward the end of World War I in the basement of a house in Yekaterinburg, but the location of their bodies was long unknown. Rumors swirled that, perhaps, some family members had escaped. In fact, a woman in Charlottesville, Virginia, insisted until her dying breath that she was Anastasia, the tsar's youngest daughter. In 1979, however, an archaeologist discovered human remains near where the tsar and his family had been killed. Scientists recovered DNA from the remains, as well as samples from blood relatives, including Prince Philip, the Duke of Edinburgh and the husband of Queen Elizabeth II, who shared a maternal lineage with the tsar back to Queen Victoria. They got a match and concluded that the remains were in fact those of the tsar and his family. They also tested the DNA of the Charlottesville woman, Anna Anderson, and concluded that she could not have been the tsar's daughter.

But what did *match* mean? Just how sure were the scientists? And how sure did they need to be to declare an identification? At first, scientists estimated that the bones discovered near Yekaterinburg had a 98.5 percent probability of belonging to the tsar and his family. Later work increased their confidence, to odds of 700 to 1 and then to nearly a million to 1.[25] These tests, plus additional DNA analysis, convinced researchers that the odds of a match could be as high as 4.36 trillion to 1.[26] That, they concluded, was good enough to declare the historical case closed. In one sense, the costs for failure were relatively low. The question was largely historical, and the tsar had no close relatives still alive. But for the historians, the issue was absolute: No one wanted to be wrong. And for companies doing DNA analysis, failure would be fatal, for a single well-publicized mistake could destroy a DNA-identification business.

In DNA typing, there are 13 DNA loci—the position of a gene on the DNA strand. The gold standard in making identifications in the United States is matching all 13. (Other countries use different standards, so the process of making identification varies by nation.) Scientists have calculated that the odds of two Caucasians matching all 13 DNA loci are astronomical: 1 in 575 trillion. With a population of humans on earth of 7 billion, such a match would seem to make identification from a match of all 13 loci a certainty. The statistical problem, however, is harder because there are two separate questions: Assessing the odds that the DNA in a set of remains comes from an individual that researchers are trying to identify, and determining the chances that two different samples match.

There is, for example, what scientists call the "birthday problem." The odds of any individual having a birthday on a particular day, leaving aside the peculiarities of the leap year, are 1 in 365. In a group of just 23 people, however, there is a 50 percent chance that two people will have the same birthday.[27] There are many cases that might seem to have huge odds against matches, but where the odds are not quite as high as they seem. Such matches complicate the problem of determining what proof is good enough to make an identification.

In a surprise to most people—but to few statisticians—investigators have discovered DNA matches in large samples of people who have nothing to do with each other. In Arizona, a crime lab investigator looked at the state's criminal DNA database. A common identification technique is to run the DNA from a crime scene against the DNA of a suspect, or to run the DNA from a crime scene sample against a panel of possible suspects. This investigator instead ran the DNA profile of convicted felons against each other, and she came up with a hit: a match on nine DNA markers (out of a possible 13) between two individuals.[28] That is, she was able to get at least modest matches of criminals with other criminals who had no connection but living under the same prison roof. If matches proved more common than was thought, how sure could investigators be about concluding that they had a match between crime scene evidence and a suspect?

Part of the answer lies in the standard for making an identification. Finding a match of nine of 13 loci was not nearly as strong a conclusion as matching all 13, and certainty increases significantly with the number of loci matches. But her research also raised caution, since discovering at least modest matches in DNA samples turned out to be easier than some analysts had suspected. Statistician Bruce S. Weir pointed out that a sample of 65,000 individuals, the number in the Arizona state crime DNA database, could produce more than 2 billion possible pairs of profiles. Matches were no more surprising with so large a number of possible pairs than finding people who share birthdays in surprisingly small groups.[29] Researchers in two other states confirmed the finding. In two states, a search for matches within the DNA databases found 1,000 matches on nine or more loci.[30] Matches on all 13 markers remains the gold standard in the United States, and the odds of a match between two unconnected people are very, very low. But they are not zero. The central problems are establishing just how sure we need to be before we act, how to know how sure we actually are, and whether more digging could make us more sure.

This is a variant of an emerging big data problem, what statisticians Persi Diaconis and Frederick Mosteller called the "law of truly large numbers." They wrote, "With a large enough sample, any outrageous thing is likely to happen." If something is so rare as to be a million-to-one shot for any individual on any day, it is likely to happen 250 times a day and 100,000 times a year. It is a commonplace that state lottery tickets are a poor investment because the odds of winning are so low. Of course, someone *does* win. However, the odds of the same person winning twice would seem impossible. Nevertheless, a New Jersey woman won the lottery twice in just a four-month span. The odds of that happening to one person were 1 in 17 trillion. Over a seven-year period, however, statisticians calculated that it is virtually a sure thing that *someone* will win twice, and that the odds were 1 in 30 that someone would win twice in a four-month period.[31] Likewise, the chance of finding two individuals in a sample of 65,000 who match on nine DNA markers was about 94 percent.[32]

MORE EVIDENCE, MORE UNCERTAINTY

Policymakers want to know things. Moneyball advocates argue that they ought to try even harder to know even more with even better evidence. But much—perhaps all—of what they really want to know is inevitably bathed in uncertainty. Some of the uncertainty is obvious, like forecasts about the weather or future unemployment trends. Some of the uncertainty can be estimated, like the chances that the DNA of a sample with human remains actually came from the same person. Some of the uncertainty lies more deeply hidden, like the birthday problem and DNA matches among prisoners. And some uncertainty lurks in what Nassim Nicholas Taleb christened the "black swan" problem: a seemingly unpredictable event that has a large but unexpected impact. After the event, explanations appear from hindsight that make it appear less random and more predictable—but not enough people predicted it with enough confidence to force action. (All swans were presumed to be white until explorers discovered black swans in Australia in the 17th century.)[33] Depending on one's reading of history, the economic crisis of 2008–09 was a prime example of the black swan problem—as was the September 11 terrorist attack.

Uncertainty surrounds everything that matters in public policy, especially the most important decisions that policymakers must make. Policymakers hunger to know what the results of their decisions will be, but they must live in the gray world of not knowing enough about the things that are most important. Learning more is always possible, but it is also always more expensive, in time and money. They must therefore focus their resources on the things that they decide matter most, both because of the importance of the decision and the consequences of being wrong. And they have to decide how much evidence is enough.

That takes us back to the core issue of evidence in public policy: gathering information *good enough* on which to take action. That, of course, is the fundamental challenge of whether more and better information can drive better results in a government increasingly interwoven. What is "good enough" varies greatly by the decision at hand. It is possible to study carefully what kind of temporary no-parking sign is most likely to survive assault by the elements, but local government officials might decide investing resources to discover what paving material will best prevent potholes is more important. For New York City's officials, it was essential to identify as many victims of the World Trade Center collapse as possible. When existing science did not supply as much help as they needed, they demanded new kinds of science to fill the gap. The scientists, of course, had already been at work improving DNA research, but the national crisis that flowed from the September 11 terrorist attacks accelerated their progress in ways that otherwise would not have happened. Evidence for making better policy decisions—in this case, using DNA analysis to identify victims—was a product both of supply, what the scientists could do, and of demand, what the policymakers needed.

The interaction of supply and demand forces has long driven advances in governments' use of information. Consider criminal investigations over the past two centuries. As table 6-1 (see page 135) shows, the demand for a better way of identifying criminals and victims drove the science; increasingly sophisticated techniques provided a far more robust supply of information that police, trial courts, and other government officials used. For example, the use of mug shots increased as photography improved. By the 1960s, new phototelemetry techniques, connecting scanned data from eyes, mouth, ears, and nose with photos on file, allowed police to use semiautomatic systems to identify individuals from photos. In the 1970s, markers like the thickness of the lips and hair color helped automate the system, and, by the 1980s, new techniques in linear algebra vastly improved identification. At the 2001 Super Bowl, investigators stunned the criminal investigation world by capturing a collection of images and matching them to a digital database.[34]

Demands for better techniques led to an ever-increasing—and better-quality—supply of information, which generated new uses. By the 2010s, police were employing these techniques to identify missing children and possible terror suspects. Airline passengers who signed up for the U.S. Customs and Border Protection's Global Online Enrollment System could skip immigration lines when returning to the country. Electronic kiosks checked photos and fingerprints against the database of those who had registered for the program, in a transaction no longer than getting money from an ATM.

The use of DNA in identifying both criminals and victims spun off the Human Genome Project, launched in 1990 to map the genes that make up the human body. The National Institutes of Health and the U.S. Department of Energy managed the project, and, by the time it was completed in 2003, it involved researchers not only in the United States but also in China, France, Germany, Japan, and the United Kingdom.[35] Once scientists completed the basic research in mapping the human genome, applications spun off quickly. In 1987 a Florida woman's home was burglarized, and the burglar raped the woman at knifepoint. Investigators matched DNA taken at the crime scene with blood drawn from a suspect, Tommie Lee Andrews. Andrews claimed he had been at home the night of the attack, but prosecutors used the DNA evidence to convince jurors that Andrews committed the crime. Assistant State Attorney Tim Berry convinced jurors that there was only a 1 in 10 billion chance that someone else would have the same DNA fragments, and the jurors were convinced.[36] Andrews was convicted and sentenced to 22 years in prison.

Table 6-1. Accelerating Innovations in Techniques for Collecting Evidence in Criminal Cases

YEAR	INNOVATION
1840s	Belgian police use photos to track criminals
1901	Scotland Yard adopts fingerprint identification system
1960s	Scientists develop semiautomatic system to identify faces from photos
1987	In the first criminal conviction based on DNA evidence, Tommie Lee Andrews is convicted of rape in Florida and sentenced to a 22-year sentence.
1995	Despite a large amount of DNA evidence, O. J. Simpson is acquitted of murder, in part because his defense raised doubts about the collection and analysis of DNA samples.
1997	Bode Technology partners with the Commonwealth of Virginia to use DNA to investigate cold cases.
2000	DNA used to identify 860 remains from 88 victims of Alaska Airlines crash.
2001–04	Improved DNA techniques used to identify more than 800 victims from more than 8,000 remains at the World Trade Center.

Source: Based on Michael Parker Banton, "Police," *Encyclopedia Britannica* (www.britannica.com/topic/police), and the author's research.

At the time of the Andrews trial, there was no national database to use in matching DNA samples. In 1990 the FBI began developing CODIS, the Combined DNA Index System, which allowed investigators to search for matches with individuals in a national database. Meanwhile, detectives vastly expanded the use of DNA matching in criminal investigations. The 1995 trial of O. J. Simpson for the murder of his former wife, Nicole Brown Simpson, and Ronald Goldman catapulted DNA into the national spotlight. Police investigators found blood samples at the murder scene, in Simpson's car, on his socks, and on a pair of gloves. They conducted DNA typing on the evidence—45 samples in all—and they testified that they found blood from the victims on the socks, glove, and car and found Simpson's own blood at the crime scene. The case seemed foolproof until one of Simpson's attorneys, Barry Scheck, systematically attacked the investigative team. The samples had remained in a hot truck for hours, which might have degraded the samples. The criminalist doing the DNA typing could not assure jurors that he had changed gloves after handling each sample, so it was possible that DNA samples had been cross-contaminated. It was not so much an attack on the value of the DNA evidence but on how it was collected, but that weakened jurors' confidence in the DNA evidence enough to win an acquittal. As *Los Angeles Times* columnist Pat Morrison wrote later, "We had a twenty-first century technology and nineteenth century evidence collection methods."[37] It was a tactic that played directly into the broader defense strategy of distrusting the police, and it worked.

The case led to a searching reexamination not only of the methods of DNA identification but also of how best to present it. By the time Bode Technology began its partnership with Virginia in 1997, DNA identification had moved far beyond the embarrassment of the Simpson case. It evolved from a novel to a trusted method, and it moved past the case-by-case approach to one that allowed matches on a larger scale. By the time of the Alaska Airlines crash in 2000, DNA identification by matching remains with samples was ready for large-scale use, and that prepared the way for the enormous expansion that the September 11 terrorist attacks required. New technologies created new demands from decision makers, and decision makers' demands stimulated the research needed to increase the supply. The incredible pressures for identifying September 11 victims sparked new insights and innovations. In just a few months, investigators moved from identifying fewer than a hundred victims of the plane crash from hundreds of remains to identifying many hundreds of victims from the thousands of remains recovered. Tremendous demand-side pressures from the attacks generated new scientific advances that, in turn, vastly increased the supply of data.

DISTORTING DEMAND, SUPPRESSING SUPPLY

Balancing the supply and demand of evidence, however, is not always a straightforward transaction. Evidence has value only to the degree to which it is used, and *how* users employ it shapes the incentives of those who produce it. There are powerful forces that can distort the demand for information, suppress its supply, and lead to misuse—or nonuse—of information.

The more data and evidence become important, the higher the incentives to game the way data are created and interpreted. Consider a case in New York City, where a police officer, concerned about police misbehavior, wore a wire for 17 months while on the job in Brooklyn's Bedford-Stuyvesant neighborhood. It is a fascinating portrait of life on the front lines of a particularly rough precinct. The tapes, shared with a reporter for the *Village Voice*, capture what the officer said were pressures to make a quota of arrests but to downplay the reports of some crimes to improve the picture of the city's crime.[38] The tape captures a borough commander pushing officers to boost their "activity"—or "paying the rent," as the cops called it. "If you don't want to work, then, you know what, just do the old go-through-the-motions and get your numbers anyway," he said. A sergeant underlined the point. "They are looking at these numbers, and people are going to get moved," he said. "It ain't about losing your job. They can make your job real uncomfortable, and we all know what that means": less-desirable assignments and no support for promotions. A lieutenant sympathized: "This job is just getting tighter and tighter with accountability." He added, "So there are certain things I'd like to get away with, but I can't anymore. It just goes down the line, and, eventually, it falls on you."

In addition to strong pressure to run up some numbers, the officer also charged that cops were being pushed to reduce the severity of charges. Referring to the "61," the department's form for collecting information about crimes, a fellow cop told him, "A lot of 61s—if it's a robbery, they'll make it a petty larceny. I saw a 61, at T/P/O [time and place of occurrence], a civilian punched in the face, menaced with a gun, and his wallet was removed, and they wrote 'lost property.'" In the course of investigating the story, the *Village Voice* reported that the department rejected burglary claims if victims did not have receipts for the items, that felonies (for thefts over $1,000) became misdemeanors "by lowballing the value of the property," that robberies sometimes became assaults, and that assaults were reclassified as harassments.[39]

Why would cops do this? Victims sometimes exaggerate what happened for a host of reasons, from making insurance claims to getting even with someone to simply puffing up a claim, and cops are cautious about taking what a victim claims at face value. Moreover, police commanders sometimes have their own incentives to "downcode" crime reports to demonstrate that they are reducing the crime rate. Two authors, John A. Eterno and Eli B. Silverman, charged that officers manipulated the data to produce statistics that demonstrated crime was falling—and that the data were unreliable.[40] They concluded that there were "enormous pressures to decrease the numbers of index crimes [the crimes reported to the FBI and used to assess long-term crime rates] and to downgrade index crimes into other non-reported categories," which would paint a portrait of declining crime.[41] William Bratton, who served as New York police commissioner from 1994 to 1996, helped invent the CompStat process that tracked crime. When he returned as commissioner in 2014, he said simply, "Nothing could be further from the truth." He added, "One thing is abundantly clear. New York City is irrefutably a far safer place than it was 16 years ago. You can't manipulate that reality."[42]

Charges about manipulating reality, however, have swirled around other programs, as well. Federal investigators found one hospital chain where emergency department physicians were pressured to ensure that at least half of all admitted patients were over the age of 65, because their expenses could be billed to Medicare. Doctors who met the target had their names in green on the daily scorecard posted for all the physicians to see. Those close to the target had their names in yellow. For those who fell behind, the names were in red.[43] At U.S. Department of Veterans Affairs hospitals, some staffers developed an intricate system of "zeroing out the date" when patients called to request an appointment. A patient would call in to schedule a meeting. The VA representative would ask what date was convenient. If the VA's first available appointment was long after the time the patient wanted, the scheduler would cancel the first request, check to make sure the new time would work for the patient, and enter the later date as the time the patient had requested from the beginning. "So now, the official wait time was . . . a perfect zero days," reported the *Washington Post*'s David A. Fahrenthold.[44] This cooking of the books was the beginning of a major scandal that in 2014 led to the resignation of the department's secretary and plunged the enormous department into crisis.

EVIDENCE AS A POLITICAL GAME

It is hard to resist the notion that evidence produces better government—and that the only thing better would be even more evidence. After all, making decisions is the core of government. Better evidence would seem to make for better decisions; better evidence, therefore, ought to lie at the core of making government better. But this is not always true, because the use of evidence creates political games.

All evidence is political

If evidence matters, it matters because it helps shape important policy decisions and their execution. Those elements, in turn, are inevitably about politics. Different options reflect different value judgments, and choosing one over the other inevitably advances some values more than others. Evidence cannot be neutral; efforts to make it appear so only submerge the value questions in ways that make the value judgments harder to make. Therefore . . .

All evidence is gamed

Anything that can be gamed to advance some values *will* be gamed. All teachers learn this lesson in the first week they are in the classroom, when students inevitably ask, "Will this reading be on the exam?" Students invariably try to game the assignments. Smart instructors reply, "Well, it might be, and it would be wise if you complete the reading to be sure." There are powerful incentives to advance evidence that advances the values dear to the players. So . . .

Evidence, especially evidence used for compliance, creates powerful incentives for distortion

The tales from the front lines of the Bedford-Stuyvesant police precinct demonstrate that if information matters, supervisors and subordinates alike will want to advance information that puts them in the best light. If the department's goal is to demonstrate that police officers are hardworking, the incentives for writing lots of tickets and making lots of arrests are high. If the goal is to demonstrate that crime is falling, the incentives for downcoding crimes are high. This is because . . .

Decision makers tend to rely most on information they find useful

As Charles E. Lindblom and David K. Cohen begin in their wonderful little book *Usable Knowledge*, "In public policy making, many suppliers and users of social research are dissatisfied, the former because they are not listened to, the latter because they do not hear much they want to listen to."[45] Only information that satisfies users—evidence that feeds the demand side—satisfies this need. But to feed demand, there must be a supply of the kind of evidence decision makers want. Too often, we supply information that has no audience. In addition . . .

Decision makers do not need to rely on systematic evidence at all in making and executing policy

Not only is much systematic evidence unused because it fails to satisfy the needs of decision makers; decision makers often decide without systematic evidence at all. As we saw at the beginning of this chapter, there is information of some kind about anything that matters. Decision makers often find it easier to take what is administratively handy and politically convenient rather than wrestling with the complexities of truly systematic evidence. There are many sources of information other than scientifically tested evidence. Moreover . . .

Reliance on evidence can paradoxically undermine government's legitimacy

The accumulation of administrative procedures and the collection of information, Francis Fukuyama wrote in his masterpiece, *Political Order and Political Decay*, can actually weaken government. These formal procedures "are designed to increase accountability and therefore the democratic legitimacy of decision making. But they also multiply rules, impose large transaction costs, and slow government action." As a result, administrators can lose the autonomy they need to do their jobs. Moreover, Fukuyama argues, "If demands for accountability become just another weapon in partisan political combat, they will not achieve their purpose." Instead, they can create a system "based more on fear than loyalty," a system that presumes government officials "cannot be trusted to do their jobs in the absence of careful external monitoring." The result, he wrote, is that "procedures, designed to increase accountability and therefore legitimacy, have the ultimate impact of making the government less effective." That, he concluded, could "paradoxically undercut its legitimacy."[46] The lesson is clear. The value of evidence depends on the purpose to which it is put.

There is a powerful instinct, rooted both in the quest for knowledge and in the analytical reflex, that if we know more, we can make better decisions. That is undoubtedly true. But getting more and better evidence does not necessarily improve public policy unless it satisfies both the supply and demand sides for information.

EVIDENCE AS AN OPERATIONAL PUZZLE

The pursuit of better evidence is actually an effort to bring two different kinds of information to bear on government's decisions. One is stronger analysis about the decisions: How can the government use evidence about the results of past decisions to make better ones? The other is stronger analysis about management: How can the government use evidence about implementation strategies to improve the results it produces? On a broad level, these are, of course, interrelated questions about how we can use evidence to make government work better. In practice, however, weaving these two kinds of evidence together often proves very difficult.

When it comes to improving decisions, the gold standard for evidence is the randomized control trial. As in tests of new drugs, researchers divide subjects randomly into two groups and analyze whether the treatment—in this case, a government program—makes a significant difference. Researchers across the world have urged a far stronger focus on this approach, because it provides the best evidence on which policy decisions produce the best results. A white paper produced by the British government could not be more direct. Its authors conclude, "Randomised controlled trials (RCTs) are the best way of determining whether a policy is working."[47]

But not everyone agrees. It is not so much that they do not believe evidence matters or that randomized control trials are valuable. It is that they are looking at different kinds of questions, involving different actors doing different things over different periods of time. Some analysts and practitioners focus not only on which management strategies produce the best results but how managers can adjust and fine-tune those strategies in real time. Randomized control trials are expensive, complex, and time-consuming, especially if researchers want to wait long enough to ensure that what they are observing is truly the result of the programmatic intervention. Public managers often want to know instead just what changes they can make to improve results. As Robert D. Behn points out, "The trial does not tell you *how* the policy works. It doesn't tell you *what* caused the improvement. And this may make it difficult to adapt the policy to different circumstances."[48] That, Behn concludes, can best come from performance management, the ongoing effort to assess how management strategies affect results—and how management improvements can produce better results.

The questions, of course, are interrelated. But the evidence examining them rarely becomes linked in practice, for several reasons.

Different methods for different questions

Randomized control trials can provide evidence on what broad *policy decisions* are most likely to produce the best results. Performance management can provide evidence on which *implementation steps* are most likely to produce which results. These are different approaches, focused on different questions.

Different time frames

Randomized control trials assess results over a long period, often many years. Performance management assesses implementation strategies over a short period, often days or weeks. The different time horizons are often difficult to link.

Different disciplines

Analysts who conduct randomized control trials are often trained as economists or statisticians. Performance management is typically conducted by those trained in public management. Even though the questions are closely related, the different disciplinary bases often create communication barriers because the information is sent and received through different disciplinary lenses.

Different organizational bases

The bureaucratic homes creating the two kinds of analyses are often different. Randomized control trials often emerge from central budget offices or policy evaluation units (which themselves are often staffed by economists or statisticians). Performance management often comes from central management organizations or operational units. Rarely do these organizational bases connect.

Different audiences

The two kinds of analyses often go to different audiences. Randomized control trials seek to inform high-level policy decisions, especially by legislators and top-level executives. On the other hand, although top executives often participate in performance management meetings—that was the case for New York City's CompStat, Baltimore's CitiStat, and Maryland's StateStat—the action for performance management happens at the operational level. There is often a large, sometimes unbridgeable, distance between the two.

EVIDENCE, GOING FORWARD

Thus, not all evidence is the same. It often speaks to different questions, time frames, disciplines, organizations, and audiences. And that frames the central dilemma. If more evidence is the key to improving government in the information age, how can we bridge these divides?

Improved technology can drive better information and evidence, but it can also lead to better service delivery. Virtually all governments have moved to online portals to provide information about government programs. Most allow citizens to conduct much of their business on the Internet without having to visit government offices, from renewing motor vehicle registrations to paying the water and sewer bill. Citizens can file formal complaints. Many cities have instituted 311 services, which allow citizens to call in with service requests. (The most frequent requests in Chicago: broken streetlights, graffiti, garbage can problems, and rats.)[49] Goldsboro, North Carolina, created a geographic information system link to its 311 call service so citizens could track problems, from potholes to illegal dumping, in any part of the city.[50] In Montgomery County, Maryland, residents can use the web to track the government's progress in plowing neighborhood streets before they venture out after a storm.[51] And a 2014 study by the National Academy of Public Administration anticipated that the Social Security Administration could use technology to reduce the demand for face-to-face meetings to deal with the Baby Boom avalanche and improve service when the service's employees talk with citizens. The report anticipated that, just as citizens can conduct much of their financial business with banks, credit card companies, and investment firms online, they could do the same for their business with government agencies.[52]

Technology offers other opportunities for citizens to forge new partnerships with government. Code for America, a nonprofit organization, created open-source apps, including "Adopt-A-Hydrant," which citizens could use to sign up for a hydrant in their neighborhood and agree to dig it out after a heavy snowstorm. Too often, firefighters rolled up to a fire only to find the hydrant buried under piles of snow. The program, with its app, helped firefighters shave precious minutes off their response time.[53] That proved especially handy in the middle of Boston's epic snowstorms in the winter of 2015.[54] Another app, "Aunt Bertha," allows citizens to type in their zip code to track down health, food, job training, and housing programs in their area. Computer code writers and app builders hope they can improve service delivery and make government more creative. They also hope to bring greater transparency and a stronger connection between citizens and government.

Amid all the uncertainty about government's future, there is one sure thing. It will operate in a world of increasing technology and data. The question is not whether government will use technology more. The puzzles, rather, are what form that use will take, whether government will lead or lag in the advancement of technology, and the degree to which this technology will fuel more use of evidence to improve government decisions and execution.

More information, more transparency, and more technology are all attractive—but they are also inherently threatening. Moreover, they are not politically neutral. English philosopher Francis Bacon coined the phrase *scientia potestas est* (knowledge is power) in 1597. Because power and politics are interconnected, all knowledge in government has political meaning. And because we cannot ever know everything, and because we do not know what we do not know, the puzzle of how to act on knowledge inevitably is loaded with debates over values. Finally, because knowledge is loaded with values, we cannot consider the role of evidence in government as an inherently good or politically neutral thing. That means suggesting the use of more evidence will create winners, losers, and new games to help the winners win more and the losers lose less.

It is a truism that government will have more information in the future to guide its action. The real question is how it will use that information: more systematic and aggressive use of information, evidence, and technology by government—or less. Reformers, like the Moneyball team, believe fervently that more evidence is preferable. But given the political principles of information that we explored earlier in this chapter, it is surely possible to see a government awash in more information—and a government that does not use that information well. Determining just how government will use the tides of information that are rising, and whether it can marshal that information to deal with the challenges of an interwoven government in the information age, is the fundamental challenge of managing 21st-century government. Indeed, in a system of governance ever more interwoven between government and its nongovernmental partners, command and control can never work to ensure high performance. We need a different tool to bridge the boundaries. In the information age, better information is the key to whether government can leverage the work of its partners. We turn to different scenarios about how that might happen in chapter 7.

SEVEN

Leveraged Government

S TEVE PALLADINO ONCE RAN AN ice-cream shop on Centre Street in West Roxbury, Massachusetts. His store, iScream Works, was "the best ice cream shop in Boston hands down," one patron wrote on Yelp.[1] But above the store, Palladino conducted a different kind of business. His company, Viking Financial Group, took in money from friends and business associates in exchange for promises of big returns. In reality, Palladino ran a Ponzi scheme that bilked dozens of investors out of more than $10 million.

It is an old fraud, made famous by Charles Ponzi's notorious scheme in the 1920s. An operator sets up shop, takes in money, pays off old investors with new investors' money, enjoys a lavish life, and eventually runs out of new pigeons to pay off new recruits. In March 2013 Palladino's operation came tumbling down when government investigators discovered his plot and indicted him for larceny and loan sharking.[2]

The Massachusetts state police made the bust, but officials in the Boston office of the Securities and Exchange Commission (SEC) pulled the evidence together. The SEC was one of the robust products of the Progressive era—an independent regulatory agency created in 1934 and charged with cleaning up abuses in the capital markets that helped trigger the Great Depression. It has long been an agency of great power and real professionalism, but it is also an agency facing huge challenges. Financial investments are increasingly complex, the Internet makes it easier to create new scams, and it is harder to recruit smart young employees to take on the intricate details of government auditing and financial oversight. At a May 2015 congressional committee hearing, Senator Heidi Heitkamp (D-N.D.) interrupted the usual questioning of witnesses to talk with a group of students who had stopped in to watch the hearing. "I am tempted to ask them how many of you want to be an IRS auditor," she said. After looking around, she concluded, "Nope, none of them."[3] To be fair, most kids do not grow up dreaming about auditing taxes or investigating securities fraud. Some kids do, however, grow up with larceny in their hearts, and society has little chance of evening the odds if it cannot hire smart government workers to even the odds.

In this case, though, the SEC was lucky to have recruited Sofia Hussain. After earning an MBA from the London School of Economics in 2010, the SEC hired her as a forensic accountant who did for securities fraud what CSI investigators do for crime scenes. Her office became the repository for enormous stacks of bankers boxes, filled with more than 35,000 pieces of paper from subpoenas of Palladino's banks. The SEC's traditional approach to such evidence had long been to wade through the paper, one sheet at a time. After the dawn of computers, SEC employees would add an additional step: typing the information by hand into spreadsheets. "Paper was just the way it was always done," Hussain explained. After all, it had worked for a long time. The SEC got its convictions, and shipping reams of paper had always been the way private banks responded to federal subpoenas.

But there were two big problems with the "this is the way we have always done it" approach. It took a lot of expensive staff time to enter and sort out the data—and the longer it took, the easier it was for some of the assets to slip away. Every dollar lost was a dollar that could not be returned to those that scammers bilked of their money.

Hussain and her colleagues asked the sensible question: If bank depositors for years had been able to download their bank statements onto their computers and then use software like Quicken to analyze them, why couldn't the federal government switch from paper documents to machine-readable data? The SEC bought new software that converted the 35,000 sheets of paper to machine-readable spreadsheets in just three hours, instead of asking its staff to take months hand-entering the data. Then the SEC negotiated with the banks to change the age-old system of responding to subpoenas with piles of paper to supplying electronic data, so that the feds had access to the bank account data in the same way that individual depositors typically did on their home computers.

The simple switch from paper to electronic files produced an investigative miracle. In just two weeks of hard work, Hussain and her colleagues determined how much cash Palladino had collected, where he had stashed the cash, and what eventually happened to it. Palladino had told his investors that he was running a lending operation, making loans at high rates of interest and then sharing his returns with investors. Hussain found no substantial lending business. The cash instead went for vacations, cars, gambling, education for Palladino's kids, and gifts for his mistress. He was a "casino whale," betting heavily enough that Caesars flew him from Boston to Atlantic City in a private jet.[4] The evidence Hussain and her colleagues assembled proved so powerful that Palladino pled guilty in exchange for a ten-year sentence. The SEC tracked down the investments they could find and, because of the speed of the investigation, they were able to return some money to those Palladino had swindled. One victim was not so lucky. Among the last investors into the scheme was the grandmother of one of Palladino's closest friends. She thought she was turning her life savings into a larger investment to leave to her grandchildren. Her money disappeared.

It is good public policy to prevent bad guys from stealing the life savings of grandmothers. Catching the bad guys faster, reclaiming more of the money, and creating stronger warnings for those who might consider doing the same thing in the future is even better policy. And we surely want to do even more of this. Hussain's work is a model of how it can work. Like virtually all government problems that matter, her work on the Palladino case was interwoven with state officials and private banks. But the two big breakthroughs in this case were the SEC's recruitment of a new generation of tech-savvy investigators and new strategies for bringing better evidence and data to bear through leveraged government. It is a hopeful sign, and it frames the propositions about government that lie ahead.

PROPOSITIONS SHAPING THE FUTURE

Predicting the future of governance in America is a difficult proposition. As one of America's great philosophers, former New York Yankees catcher Yogi Berra, put it, "It's tough to make predictions, especially about the future." Six propositions, however, are good bets for the future of government's search for competence.

1. American government is not likely to get less ambitious. Citizens' expectations about what government ought to do have increased over the past century. So has the political instinct of politicians, Republicans and Democrats alike, to respond. The Tea Partiers and libertarians have pressed to reverse the steady march of government's reach, but there is little support for fundamentally peeling back government's role. More than two dozen Republican members of Congress voted against storm relief for victims of Superstorm Sandy in 2013 but separately requested federal aid to help victims of other disasters in their own states.[5] How much aid the federal government ought to provide for which kinds of disasters is a fair debate. An even more important puzzle is how best to bend down the cost curve for the government's disaster relief programs. As the debate over the Sandy relief package showed, it is unlikely that members of Congress will stop seeking help for their own citizens when disaster strikes— or when other problems threaten. Citizens expect that government will solve their problems, and that is not going to change.

2. Government's interweaving of work across the boundaries of governance is not likely to shrink. There is a rhetorical dilemma in preaching restraint while extending government's reach, of course. It is a dilemma that Progressives of both parties recognized a long time ago and tried to solve by putting tight boundaries around government's action. But there is a limit to how much government's reach can expand without growing government itself. And, when policymakers hit that wall, they found it far more politically attractive and pragmatically effective to increase government's role by weaving its activities throughout the nongovernmental world. That understandably confuses everyone about who is in charge of what and makes it hard to hold anyone ultimately accountable. The confusion often benefits policymakers. If responsibility for results is broadly shared, it is tough to hold anyone responsible for any problems. It is far easier for liberals to expand government's reach if government itself does not have to be expanded; it is easier for conservatives to stomach a broader governmental role if it happens through nongovernmental partners; and it is easier for both parties to stage political attacks on the other when problems occur. Interweaving is not likely to shrink, because it works for both parties.

3. The quantity of information will surely grow. There has never been a time when we have had more information about government and its operations, and there is no sign the trend is going to slacken. In 1991 Oregon launched a statewide effort to track 158 indicators about the quality of life and government.[6] Since 1994, New York City's police department has been tracking patterns of crime and which police strategies work best for reducing it. The U.S. Departments of Housing and Urban Development and Veterans Affairs developed a data system to reduce the homelessness of veterans.[7] These programs—and more— generated huge volumes of data. In fiscal year 2013 the Office of Management and Budget estimated that the public spent 9.45 billion hours providing information to the federal government, an 18 percent increase over the previous decade. About three-fourths of the burden came from taxpayers' struggle to comply with the tax code. Accounting for much of the rest were the Departments of Health and Human Services (for paperwork filed to support Medicare and Medicaid payments) and Transportation (including documentation of the work of long-distance truckers, the safety of trains, and the maintenance of aircraft), the SEC (for financial filings on stocks and bonds), the Environmental Protection Agency (for documentation of compliance with clean air, water, and soil standards), and the Department of Labor (for documentation of compliance with workplace rules).[8]

4. But we often do not have enough of the right data. In "Moneyball for Government," John Bridgeland and Peter Orszag argued that we do not know enough of the right things to improve government. We are plagued, they said, by "failing to measure the impact of so many of our government programs."[9] Some government programs not only do not work—they make things worse, but we often fail to pay attention to information showing the extent of failures we continue to fund. Perhaps the most famous example is the "Scared Straight" program, which launched in New Jersey, spread around the country, and became popular in the perennially highly rated television show *Beyond Scared Straight*. The idea is simple. Take young offenders behind bars to see what hard-core prison life is like, with the hope that once they experience the world behind bars they will be scared straight. The evidence, derived from randomized control trials, shows otherwise. Not only do "scared straight" programs fail to lead kids away from crime—the programs actually seem to produce better criminals. Crimes committed by those enrolled in the programs increased in all the states a team of analysts studied. In Michigan, delinquency increased by 26 percent.[10]

5. *Much of the information collected simply goes to demonstrate compliance with rules rather than to improve the delivery of programs.* A quick look at the information collected by government reveals that much of it supports box-checking compliance with government requirements. Rules that demand changes in behavior require information to prove that behavior changes. Behavior changes are never easy, so it is tempting for citizens and government officials alike to use the information to get compliance monitors off their backs. For many players in government's world, that means information is often viewed as a gotcha game, to identify problems, or as defense against investigations, to minimize hassles. And that, in turn, makes it harder to convince all the players to use information to support positive steps like making programs work better, because many government insiders look on information with profound suspicion.

6. *Whether we like it or not, we need an information-age government.* Hussain's approach to the Boston Ponzi scheme certainly demonstrates the kind of government we want: information-driven, innovation-based, and staffed by smart employees who can keep the government a step ahead of the bad guys and help defend the good guys. No one wants to see a grandmother's life savings evaporate behind a scheming wall of fraud. Michigan Governor Rick Snyder put the question sharply. "Government started getting involved in people's lives, and it was needed," he explained. As the years went by, however, we have grown into "a massive accumulation of prescriptive programs largely led by the federal government. That's not a model that works well anymore. . . . We're not treating people as people, the way they deserve."[11] If that is not the future we want, how can we get to where we want to go?

ALTERNATIVE FUTURES: INTERWEAVING
AND EVIDENCE

The Palladino case frames the two big questions facing American governance in the 21st century. First, as government's role evolves, how much more *interweaving* will occur? The evidence from the 20th century is that government's size, reach, impact—its interweaving—has ratcheted up over time. Wars, in particular, have boosted its spending and its interconnections with nongovernmental partners. In the years after the world wars, government spending eased back, but its interweaving did not. The imperatives of war fighting drove the case for using the Progressives' argument for a stronger government; the pragmatism of doing what had to be done made it possible to grow government outside the Progressives' boundaries on governmental power. We ended up with a government out of sync: a larger government first rationalized by national security, then expanded to meet new domestic policy demands, but which failed to build the capacity to be effective or the boundaries to be accountable. That defines the first big question: Will new solutions to new problems create relatively more or less interweaving to deal with new challenges?

As government copes with these policy challenges, will it rely relatively more or less on evidence and information? Government, like every other institution and, for that matter, like every citizen, will be increasingly swamped by tsunamis of information. There will be no real choice about whether to deal with it. The question, rather, is *how*: whether government will use more evidence to drive better decisions and stronger results for citizens. This is not only a question of dealing with the flood of information produced by the information age. It is also a puzzle about whether government will use information to bridge the boundaries created by the interweaving of policy strategies. That frames the second big question: Can evidence and information build bridges across the boundaries of these interwoven strategies?

Figure 7-1. Scenarios for 21st-Century Government

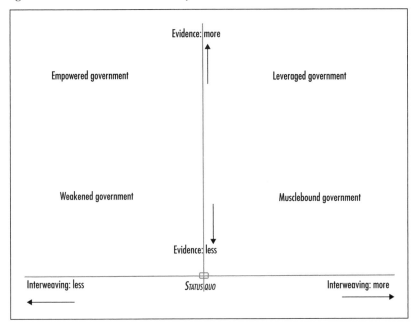

And can more reliance on information create a new system of accountability to replace the reliance on boundaries that fell out of sync with the operating realities of governance?

These two big questions—how much more interweaving, and how much reliance on information and evidence—frame four scenarios for American governance in the 21st century (see figure 7-1). Will government slow the growth of interweaving and rely relatively less on evidence, which could lead to a *weakened government*? Will the pace of interweaving increase, with government relying relatively more on evidence, which could lead to an *empowered government*? Will the pace of interweaving be less with relatively little reliance on evidence, which could lead to a *musclebound government*? Or will both interweaving and the use of evidence grow, which could lead to a *leveraged government*? Consider the tensions shaping the debate.

Interweaving

As government faces new challenges, there could be relatively *less* interweaving of government bureaucracies with the rest of society (and with the rest of the globe). Conservatives could win their battles to shrink government's size. As government shrinks, so too would its interconnection with the rest of society. Government's boundaries could be pushed back. On the other hand, liberals could continue their push to expand government by growing government itself. The Affordable Care Act could become a beachhead from which liberals achieve a single-payer health care system, like the British National Health Service. Any of these issues could shrink government's interweaving with the nongovernmental world by making government's role more direct, either in a smaller government or in a larger government managed more directly by the government's own employees.

There could also be *more* interweaving of government into the nongovernmental world. For example, citizens might insist on stronger governmental responses to more emerging problems, but they could also continue to oppose "big government" and, therefore, oppose expanding government's direct role. Cyberattacks, either from faceless enemies or foreign states, could generate calls for more powerful government protection of infrastructure (such as power plants), finances (such as credit cards and bank accounts), and commerce (such as online purchases, including Amazon or the iTunes store), which could lead to a stronger government role in the private sector. Another Hurricane Katrina or Superstorm Sandy could reinforce demands for government help in rebuilding, in exchange for a stronger governmental role in deciding who gets to rebuild where, which could increase the federal government's role in local zoning and land use decisions. Unsafe auto parts, such as the airbags manufactured by Takata during the 2000s, could lead citizens to insist on tougher safety standards. A major terrorist attack could ratchet up federal strategies to protect citizens. Stronger support for social goals could lead to more funding of faith-based and other nonprofit organizations. Any—or all—of these strategies could increase government's interweaving in the nongovernmental world.

Then there is the pragmatic case for relying more on direct governmental action, with a beefed-up government bureaucracy, to save money and improve results. Indeed, in *Bring Back the Bureaucrats*, the invariably thoughtful political scientist John DiIulio has called for the federal government to hire a million more bureaucrats by 2035 to bring more of government's work back into government.[12] That is a relatively modest bump of 50,000 new workers each year. DiIulio's bold plan has drawn attack from conservatives like Charles Murray, who contends that government's problems "are not the result of a federal workforce too small for the important tasks it has been assigned, but a federal government that has reached an advanced stage of sclerosis."[13] But one could imagine that DiIulio's case for bringing back the bureaucrats will succeed because reformers conclude it is better and cheaper for government workers to do government's work than for government to struggle with the increasingly complex world of government's proxies.

For example, the Project on Government Oversight (POGO), a Washington-based think tank, concluded in 2011 that work performed by government employees was less expensive than that done by private contractors in 33 of the 35 areas it examined. Moreover, POGO concluded, "the federal government has failed to determine how much money it saves or wastes by outsourcing, in-sourcing, or retaining services, and has no comprehensive system for doing so."[14] Defense Secretary Robert Gates said in 2010 that work done by government employees costs 25 percent less than that done by contractors.[15] However, a report for Washington's Center for Strategic and International Studies disagreed, concluding that evidence for cost savings from in-sourcing was largely anecdotal, good analysis was fragmentary, and uncertainties about the supply of work might drive up the cost among defense contractors.[16] GAO has found that good comparisons about public and private costs have been elusive.[17] We don't know for sure how much government would save if it did more of its work itself, if it would save any money at all.

The debate about the size of government—and just how much government should be done by government itself—will continue to be fierce. Cost comparisons between government and its non-governmental partners are difficult politically because every comparison is an implicit attack on contractors eager to defend their businesses and their jobs, and economically because creating comparisons that capture differences in wages, fringe benefits, and the costs of operations can prove extremely challenging. But it is at least plausible that, regardless of its size, government will decide to bring more of its work back inside government. That would produce a government with less interweaving.

Evidence

It is impossible to imagine a future in which there is *less* evidence and information about government programs. Information is growing at an astounding, virtually unmeasurable rate, and American government is one of the greatest information-generators that the world has ever seen. Article I, Section 2, of the Constitution requires the federal government to conduct a census every ten years to apportion seats in the House of Representatives, and from that foundation the flood of information on virtually everything has been a growing tsunami. There is no chance that the government will produce less information in the future, and there is no chance that government will have to deal with a smaller pile of information being generated in society and around the world.

Creating an enormous supply of information, however, does not mean that the government will use it. Many reports are printed but not read; some are read but not acted upon. Information has long existed as a tool to enforce accountability and compliance. David

Osborne and Ted Gaebler's 1993 manifesto, *Reinventing Government*, saw public organizations as obsessed with compliance with rules and sought to help them break free.[18] More recently, a 2015 Urban Institute report on the Head Start program sought to move "beyond a culture of compliance to a culture of continuous improvement."[19] The challenge is not so much increasing the supply of information. It is figuring out what evidence decision makers want, what they will use, and what will prove most persuasive.

As we saw in chapter 6, government's use of evidence and information is, at its core, a political game, with an enormous number of pressures and counter-pressures. The Moneyball argument makes the powerful case for more evidence that informs policymakers more about what works. As Michele Jolin wrote in her book, "If we can bridge that gap between knowing what needs to be done and elected officials and policymakers using that information to make better choices, then we can make great leaps in the results government gets from its investments."[20] But the road from making the argument to figuring out how to follow it, through the vastly complex counter-pressures throughout the political system, is a deceptively difficult one that exhortation cannot navigate. It is easy to imagine a case where there are more demands for more evidence, that more evidence emerges, but that those who supply the information do not meet the demands of those who would use it.

That frames the scenarios for the use of evidence in government. The sure bet is that there will be much more information. Government could find a new equilibrium in balancing the supply of information with the demand for it, and it could make far better use of evidence in making and implementing decisions. Or it could go through the motions, collecting more data but hiding behind it. It could use information to demonstrate compliance with laws, rules, and procedures, and it could use information to reinforce political judgments produced independently of the evidence. It is probable that there will be more interweaving of government with the nongovernmental world, but it is far harder to predict how much more government will create and make use of evidence in the information age.

CHARTING THE SCENARIOS

These two big forces—interweaving and evidence—frame the four scenarios about government's future. It is unlikely, of course, that we will fall neatly into one of these scenarios. The coming years are more likely to produce a hybrid. But even if the fit isn't neat, it's likely that these two forces will shape the future of American government. How policymakers balance these forces will depend on citizens' expectations about what they want government to do and how well they think government will perform.

There is a vast reservoir of polling on these questions, from both the Right and the Left. One especially interesting analysis came from Republican pollster Whit Ayres, who has worked for many candidates, including 2016 presidential candidate Marco Rubio. He pointed to a 2013 survey by the Kaiser Family Foundation, which found that 79 percent of Americans believe "it is possible for the federal government to be run well." However, he concludes, "The problem is that they do not think it is being run well now." He pointed to polls that concluded most Americans disapprove of the job Congress is doing, that 52 percent think that the federal government has a mainly negative impact on their lives, and that 55 percent of Americans give the federal government a grade of C, D, or F (with just a quarter grading it an A or a B). Given such findings, he asks, "Why would Americans want to give the federal government more authority over their lives?" The answer: "They don't." In fact, Ayres writes, when Americans are asked to consider how much government they are willing to pay for, "Americans consistently prefer a smaller government with fewer services and lower taxes to a larger government with more services and higher taxes."[21] After looking at all the polling data, Ayres concludes, "On the defining issue of the philosophy and role of government,

America remains a center-right country. Support for the center-right values of individual liberty, free enterprise, limited government, personal responsibility, and expanded opportunity remains robust in the American electorate of the 21st century."[22]

Liberals might quarrel with his political advice and his label for the electorate. But Ayres has sized up well the expectations that Americans have of their government. If Americans want a smaller government with fewer services, the missing piece of the debate is what services Americans are willing to do without. There surely are strong pressures to cut government, but there is no consensus on what government to slash because most people want the government they have. In 2013, amid one of the periodic congressional budgetary standoffs, the Pew Research Center surveyed Americans about what programs they would want to cut. In their review of 19 programs, there was a majority only for cutting programs to needy people around the world: 48 percent favored cutting these programs, 28 percent keeping it the same, and 21 percent increasing it. For every other program, ranging from unemployment and defense to Social Security and veterans' benefits, there was more support for at least keeping spending at the same level than for cutting—or even increasing spending.[23] Ayres might be right that Americans want a smaller government, but there is no road map for getting there.

Americans believe that government *can* work, but they do not think it does. They think that government *could* be a positive force in their lives, but they do not believe it is. They want a smaller government and lower taxes, but they cannot agree on what programs to cut. Americans are thus complicit in the government's performance problems because what they want is something no government can deliver. Moreover, these paradoxes help explain the different roads that Republicans and Democrats have taken to the decline of competence. Democrats have supported new programs but have not paid enough attention to how to deliver them. Republicans have been quietly complicit in the creation of new programs—or have been unable to stop them, but they have fought the smaller-government battle by trying to starve management capacity. Neither party has wanted to try to reconcile the cost of government programs with the means to pay for them, so both have conspired to fund them through higher debt.

These paradoxes, in turn, frame the political and economic context in which the puzzles of performance will play out: What kind of government will we face as we look toward the future? And can it better deliver the services that citizens want and expect, even if they do not always like the government delivering them? Answering these questions requires looking at the scenarios most probable to share governance in America for the 21st century.

Weakened government: Less interweaving, less evidence

This scenario anticipates relatively less effective use of evidence. That is easy to imagine. It certainly would not be because the supply of evidence shrinks—we are creating new information faster than anyone can possibly digest it. But it is possible to imagine a government that does not effectively collect, manage, and use the information it has. Administrators could rely on information for self-defense and to demonstrate compliance. Collecting and sharing more information can make managers more vulnerable by feeding political opponents with ammunition—and by losing control of the information on which they could suffer attack. Moreover, in a politically turbulent world, policymakers could rely on their instincts, which are clear and cheap, more than evidence, which can prove expensive and uncertain.

Government could also rely less on interweaving of its functions with its nongovernmental partners by doing more of its work itself. But it is quite difficult to imagine that government would significantly shrink its footprint at the same time. It is even harder to imagine given the inexorable demographic trends already in place. In a globalized world in which the United States has asserted a strong leadership role, and in a domestic arena in which citizens have developed high expectations for goods and services, especially Social Security and health care for the elderly, this scenario seems unlikely.

Musclebound government: Less evidence, more interweaving

As in the weakened government scenario, it is certainly possible to imagine that government would make relatively little effective use of the evidence upon which it can draw. Then, with pressures on government's role increasing, both domestically and internationally, it is also possible to imagine government's interweaving increasing, as well. If the demands on government are unlikely to shrink, but with political enthusiasm to increase government's power low, government could continue to increase its reach by interweaving more of its work through nongovernmental partners. Some reformers have called for solving the air-traffic control problem by privatizing it, for solving the food-safety issue by improving product labeling and self-policing, for changing the incentives for those providing Medicare and Medicaid services to reduce improper payments, for encouraging more reliance on private and foreign weather satellites, and for insisting that private companies shoulder more of the burden for cybersecurity. In this scenario, government would not go away, but it would not be on the front lines. Its primary role would be to grease the wheels of private and nonprofit action, to steer without rowing.

It is surely possible to imagine a further increase in government's interweaving. Indeed, it would only require expanding use of the policy tools that government has used since World War II to enlarge its power and reach. In fact, the path of least resistance in meeting big new challenges is to continue doing what we have been doing, in finding even more nongovernmental partners to advance government's work. It would also be the scenario that would fit the administrative gridlock into which the Democrats and Republicans have maneuvered themselves—an overreach without attention to operations by Democrats, an effort to roll back government without attention to its consequences by Republicans, and a reluctance to engage evidence about what works by both parties.

But this scenario surely would not be a happy one. It would be bad enough if it simply produced more of the performance problems of the early 2000s, but the reality is likely to be more complicated. The real story of the first decades of the 21st century is not just the struggle to make government work in the face of mounting evidence that it does not. It is the story of a growing gap between what citizens—and, indeed, even their elected officials—want from government and its ability to deliver. The musclebound scenario is not a path for continuing the status quo; it is the road to a government that increasingly finds it tough to deliver and that citizens increasingly lose faith in. The result would be a government with great responsibility and substantial power, but an inability to marshal it to produce effective results. It would be a government especially ill executed, of which the nation's founders—let alone its Progressives of more than a century ago—would scarcely be proud.

Empowered government: Less interweaving, more evidence

Government's role is unlikely to shrink, but it is possible that government might play that role more directly, as DiIulio proposes. It would tackle head-on the uneasy equilibrium into which we have stumbled: opposition to big government, an unwillingness to cut it, and the use of indirect proxy tools as a fig leaf to hide government's real size while expanding its role. DiIulio proposes to reset this scenario by recognizing what government does, by understanding the public value that government programs create, by strengthening government's capacity to deliver, and by increasing the line-of-sight accountability from government's policymakers to those who deliver government's goods and services. DiIulio contends that government would be better—more effective, more responsive, less expensive, and more accountable—if more of the work left to proxies were brought inside, with more bureaucrats hired to do the work. This is not a plan for bigger government but for a government in which government itself does far more of what citizens expect it to do.

At the same time, the flood of evidence available to improve government decisions will only increase, both through the vast increase in information and by government's more explicit efforts to exploit it. In 2013 President Obama signed an executive order requiring that "the default state of new and modernized Government information resources shall be open and machine readable," which promised an expansion of new data.[24] (Only a wonk with grounding in computer science could have massaged the term *default state* into a presidential order.) The federal government's Data.gov has become a treasure of online information. Local government 311 systems, which allow citizens to phone in and e-mail complaints, have produced huge amounts of information, from the location of potholes to the couple whose noises during intimacy most annoyed their neighbors. (In New York, that title went to a Brooklyn couple.)[25] New York City's 311 service logged 28 million contacts in 2014, which produced a staggering amount of information.[26]

Consider Baltimore's "rat rubout" program, surely one of the best-named programs in the nation. (Is anyone *not* in favor of rubbing out rats?) The city created a program to wipe out the vermin and to identify "hot spots" of rat infestations by keeping track of citizens' calls to the city's 311 telephone line. City officials then mapped the location of the calls to determine the neighborhoods with the biggest problems. Of course, there is no "department of rats" to manage the program. The creatures tend to breed in abandoned houses, live off piles of garbage, travel through sewers, and cause problems in public health. The map of rats, therefore, is a map of a problem that requires inter-agency coordination. How the map changes is a gauge of the effectiveness of that inter-agency coordination of an immensely interwoven system.

That combination of less interweaving (with more of government's work brought in-house) and more use of data (with more of government's programs tracked carefully by data) could vastly improve government's performance. It could also empower government to better deliver the services citizens pay for and expect. But it requires a level of directness that would prove tough to achieve: a direct recognition of government's expanding reach and of government's role in providing goods and services. Given the generations of drift from the Progressive agenda, in which government's growing role came through indirect, interwoven policy strategies, that degree of directness seems unlikely.

Leveraged government: More interweaving, more evidence

The forces of political gridlock and policy momentum, however, could block empowered government. Since World War II, Democrats and Republicans have both gradually slipped into an uneasy peace for a broader governmental role exercised through indirect proxy tactics. New problems are sure to emerge for which citizens will call for a governmental response. It will be easiest for government to continue to respond through standard strategies, with an uneasy reliance on proxy strategies: Government can respond without growing government itself. When the VA struggled in 2014 to provide appointments for veterans who needed care, Congress sought to cut waiting lists by providing vets with vouchers to allow them to visit private doctors and hospitals. Faced with emerging problems in managing air-traffic control, some reformers called for spinning the function off to private providers. Proxies have proven an expedient solution to satisfy demands for more government without growing government, and the momentum for these tools could well prove hard to resist. The road to more interweaving is already paved by powerful, ongoing trends.

Government could also make more and better use of evidence, as in the empowered government scenario. What would be different from the empowered scenario? Not only would government develop evidence to enhance its decisions and the management of its own agencies;

it would use evidence as a tool to build bridges to the many partners who share in the delivery of public programs. For example, New York City annually grades the sanitation of its restaurants. Patrons can check the rating in the window before they even walk through the door—and decide if they want to trust their meal to any restaurant with less than an A rating. The *New York Times* collects these ratings and posts them on its website, on an interactive map, so restaurant-goers can check out their options before heading out for a meal.[27] The site allows consumers to scan for restaurants in particular neighbor-hoods, hover over a particular location to find more detail, click to check out precisely what the food inspector found (from the temper-ature at which hot and cold food was held to the condition of the plumbing and the cleanliness of wiping cloths), and track down evi-dence of rodents. How much difference did posting the inspection grades in the windows make? In the city's first year of public posting, restaurants earning an A on their first inspection increased from 27 to 41 percent, and more restaurants are earning better grades.[28]

San Francisco was the first city to partner with Yelp in posting municipal inspection data for citizens to check on its website. Before heading out the door from home—or before heading into the restau-rant's door from the sidewalk—patrons can check online and find the restaurant's score on a scale of 1 to 100, as well as the date of the last inspection. This not only proved popular with citizens, it created a fascinating interweaving of government data with a private website and citizens' choices, to create an interconnected network of incen-tives to improve the healthfulness of the city's eateries. It proved a premier example of how leveraged government could work: the use of data to create evidence, the use of evidence to bridge the public and private sectors, and the use of this bridge for citizens to navigate the world of complex choices around them.

There are significant barriers to increasing the role of electronic resources in government. A 2015 survey found that fewer than half of Americans who use the Internet at least once a week actually want more digital service delivery from the federal government. Privacy worries, especially in the wake of the disclosure that the National Security Agency was vacuuming up enormous volumes of citizen telecommunications data, has made many citizens skittish about relying more on electronic links with government, even as smartphone apps have vastly expanded their reliance on Internet connections. In a 2015 survey, 39 percent thought it was likely that personal information would be accessed without their consent. In another survey, just 35 percent of respondents trusted the government to keep their information private. And sometimes, e-connecting with government has little support simply because it is often difficult. Fewer than half of those surveyed found what they wanted when they visited federal websites.[29]

If evidence and data are the future, making—and trusting—the connections requires more work. Some local governments have made progress on this front, especially in harnessing information collected through their 311 and other data systems, and pushing it out through smartphone portals. In Philadelphia, for example, the city provided updates on its summer meals program, where hungry citizens could find food trucks, registration information for the upcoming marathon, and how to submit graffiti complaints. As Rosetta Carrington Lue, Philadelphia's chief customer experience strategy, innovation, and technology officer, explained, "People want information, they want it now, they want it accurate and want it on their time."[30] Online systems increasingly are providing it. And, of course, such evidence can be used to guide and hold accountable the vast network of proxies on which the government relies for service delivery.

TOWARD LEVERAGED GOVERNMENT

An effective, efficient, and accountable government for the future needs to solve the fundamental problems that emerged as the Progressives' foundation of modern government became unglued. The core issue—the erosion of confidence in government itself—will not be an easy one to crack. It has built up over time and is unlikely to be solved unless government proves it can deliver its goods and services far better. On the other hand, although this step surely will not unlock political gridlock, it is a challenge to imagine rebuilding the foundations of American government unless its officials prove they can deliver on the promises they make. It is a necessary but, ultimately, insufficient condition for strengthening American government for the 21st century. It is so fundamentally necessary, in fact, that it is possible to imagine a book on the decline and fall of the American republic written early in the 22nd century that begins its assessment of America's decay with an analysis of why it lost the capacity to deliver.

I began this chapter by pointing to a prime example of the kind of government we want and need, a government already present in the leadership of government managers like Sofia Hussain. It is a government that bridges boundaries to increase its effectiveness, relies on technology to replace traditional approaches to accountability based on structures and processes, and recruits the right people with the right skills at the right places to do what must be done. This is not a hypothetical government; it is a government that already exists and could be taken to scale, with robust new systems to support its work: to use information and evidence in two ways—modernizing the original Progressive commitment to competence, and using evidence-based approaches to help government rise to the challenges of an interwoven 21st-century government.

This means that the scenarios with relatively weak reliance on evidence—the weakened government and the musclebound government scenarios—are likely to fall short of what government needs for the 21st century. As problems spill over government's boundaries into complex proxy networks, often involving nongovernmental partners, the boundary-based strategies of the original Progressive movement have fallen short. It is unlikely they can be rebuilt and, without a fresh approach to effectiveness and accountability, government's performance will fall even farther behind. That does not mean that government might not slip into one of these scenarios. In fact, muscle-bound government, with relatively more interweaving but relatively less use of evidence, is an entirely possible scenario. It would require only that government do more of what it is doing, but doing it more poorly by relying on evidence mostly to check off compliance boxes instead of improving decisions and management.

The two most powerful scenarios—empowered government and leveraged government—both depend on making more effective use of evidence. They differ in the degree to which government inter-weaves its functions with the nongovernmental world. Empowered government envisions more of government being done by govern-ment. Leveraged government would continue the rising use of prox-ies to do its work indirectly. There is much to like about empowered government. It would clarify government's role as well as its relation-ship to citizens and taxpayers. It would strengthen government's capacity to do what citizens want done. It would allow citizens to de-cide more directly just what they want it to do. But all of those steps are difficult, precisely because they require greater clarity. For better or worse—often for worse—government's role since World War II has grown by blurring its responsibilities by increasing the use of inter-weaving. As we have seen, that served the purposes of both Republi-cans and Democrats, conservatives and liberals, who have been able to find an uneasy consensus on the same strategy, for different reasons.

That leaves leveraged government as the scenario with the best out-come. It is unlikely that the uneasy strategic consensus for interweav-ing will dissolve. Citizens probably will not pull back government's role. In fact, it is entirely possible that citizens' expectations will grow, in new areas like cybersecurity and old ones like health care, and gov-ernment will respond through broader programs that are even more interwoven between the governmental and the nongovernmental worlds. That would challenge the Progressives' model of strong gov-ernment within strong boundaries even further, since the boundaries would prove increasingly permeable if they did not crack completely. If boundaries cannot ensure accountability, what will? Information and evidence provide the best options, because information can flow across boundaries in ways that governmental and bureaucratic authority cannot. In chapter 8, we explore how we can recover the commitment to competence through leveraged government.

EIGHT

Recovering the Lost Commitment to Competence

Dᴜʀɪɴɢ ᴀ ʙᴀsᴇʙᴀʟʟ ɢᴀᴍᴇ ɴᴏᴛ long ago, a color analyst politely criticized an outfielder for sprinting after a fly ball but not extending his glove to catch it. "Wow—he really had dinosaur arms on that play!" he said. The allusion was to extinct Jurassic creatures whose short arms made it impossible to grasp much. They could compensate with brawn and strong jaws, but even that did not save them from disappearing when they failed to adapt to their changing environment.

During the last half of the 20th century, American government increasingly developed dinosaur arms. It became ever more ambitious, through tools that were ever more interwoven. But as its ambition and reach expanded, its ability to grasp did not. The result was a growing gap in its capacity to do what it promised—and a declining trust of citizens in the government's ability to get things done. Like the outfielder chasing a ball he could not catch, American government developed dinosaur arms, with a government whose competence fell short of its aims. As interweaving increased, the distance between its reach and its grasp only increased.

For more than a century, we built a government with a remarkably bipartisan consensus that, when the political battles were done, the political parties would agree that government and its programs should be managed professionally and accountably. In short, the Progressives advanced a commitment to competence. In post–World War II America, however, that commitment eroded. We wanted more public programs than we wanted to pay for, so we borrowed to fund them. We wanted a more powerful government than we wanted to support, so we pushed substantial responsibility for executing public programs out of government's hands into the private and nonprofit sectors, through a vast collection of interwoven tools, without stopping to think about how to manage them well or hold them accountable. The strategy allowed Americans to satisfy their cravings, but it left us with a government increasingly out of sync with the problems we expected it to solve and out of gas in its capacity to solve them. It is little wonder that increasingly it could not perform, behave responsibly, and sustain the public's trust.

Nothing is a better example than the epic battle over the Affordable Care Act, Barack Obama's signature program. The program's website was its public face, but the administration pushed its execution deep inside the Centers for Medicare and Medicaid Services, where overworked managers did not have the time or system-design skills to manage the contractors charged with the job. The White House failed to keep its eye on the management ball to make sure the rollout would go smoothly. It was not that the job was impossible. The Office of Management and Budget's former deputy director for management, Jeff Zients, came to the rescue with a tiger team of highly skilled analysts and, in three months, got the website up and running. By then, however, the failure at launch only further undermined the public's trust in government's ability to perform. The

Republicans, meanwhile, knew they did not have enough votes to repeal the program, but they campaigned at every opportunity to kneecap the program by undermining the administration's ability to administer the law. They never produced a consensus replacement plan for the Affordable Care Act; it was politically easier to allow health insurance for everyone to emerge while continuing to attack the decisions that produced it. The Democrats' reach extended their grasp; the Republicans tried to loosen the government's ability to grab its legislated objective.

In this and in far too many other cases, Republicans and Democrats have traveled different roads to get to the same nasty spot: a government increasingly ill executed. And, as Alexander Hamilton warned in *Federalist* No. 70, "a government ill executed, whatever it may be in theory, must be, in practice, a bad government." In *Federalist* No. 68, he built the foundation for this conclusion in writing,

> Though we cannot acquiesce in the political heresy of the poet who says:
>
> > *"For forms of government let fools contest—*
> > *That which is best administered is best,"—*
>
> yet we may safely pronounce, that the true test of a good government is its aptitude and tendency to produce a good administration.

Hamilton, a far more insightful political analyst than a scholar of literature, mangled the quotation from the poet Alexander Pope, who in fact wrote, "For forms of government let fools contest; Whate'er is best administer'd is best."[1] But he got the conclusion just right: A government ill executed is, in fact, a bad government.

Making policy decisions but undermining the ability to deliver on them is, quite simply, dishonest government. A cornerstone of our separation-of-powers system is that the making of policy is the product of debate among our elected representatives, and that it is the job of the executive to carry out the policy that policymakers choose. Endless barrels of ink have been spilled in debating the theory—and the impossibility—of separating policymaking from its execution. Carl von Clausewitz famously argued, "War is the continuation of politics by other means." Policy execution is just another arena of political warfare, and the battles that were fought in policymaking naturally spill over into its implementation. But it is hard to escape the conclusion that implementation battles have become arenas for restaging the most fundamental political conflicts. As more implementation of governmental programs becomes wrapped into nongovernmental actors, there are fewer ties holding the ongoing battles to standards of accountability. Moreover, the scale of those ongoing battles has grown to the point that it is hard for citizens to know or believe what policies their government has made, and that is not the basis of an honest conversation between voters and the officials they elect.

It is bad government not to deliver on policy promises. There is a paradox between the ongoing guerrilla battles over policy in the implementation stage, on the one hand, and the wholesale neglect of the operational questions of implementation, on the other. Elected officials have managed both to insert themselves into the details of policy execution but also to take responsibility for how it actually works. For much of the time, most officials succeed in having it both ways. But at times that are unpredictable and not of their own choosing, implementation failures suddenly and brutally emerge. It might be the failure of federal agencies to respond to local hurricanes, the failure of federal agencies to deliver on a president's signature health care reform, the sudden illnesses of restaurant-goers sickened by unsafe food, or a cyberattack by a foreign country on a private movie company. It is just as likely to happen on either party's watch but, with the rise of 24-hour news channels and vast social networks, any problem anywhere can quickly become a huge problem everywhere—one that demands instant attention and effective response. Failure brings political retribution that is just as quick.

For elected officials used to pushing questions of policy execution down the chain to subordinates, it is difficult to develop the instincts for quick and effective administrative management or for strong and powerful public communication. It is hard to predict just when a Katrina response or Obamacare website debacle might happen, but the growing complexity and interconnectedness of everything makes it increasingly certain that chief executives will face challenges of just this sort. They just do not know what, when, or where. And if they fumble the response, the political fallout can be quick and disastrous. Elected executives deemphasize policy execution at their political peril.

Finally, it is bad government because it generates public distrust in political institutions. The story of the political era since the 1960s has been one of declining trust in government. Trust is a vastly complex phenomenon, and rising distrust is certainly not just an American pathology. In the United States, the roots lie in everything from crises such as Vietnam and Watergate to presidential dissembling to rising economic security and growing income inequality to intractable gridlock. No one problem is at the core; no one solution can end the problem. Nevertheless, it is clear that large and ongoing problems in delivering public programs, in an efficient and accountable manner, are making the problems of distrust even worse.

The Progressives surely did not have it all right, but they did succeed in building a bipartisan coalition among Republicans and Democrats behind a singular notion: Whatever the policy idea, citizens deserved a program that was competently administered. That consensus gradually evaporated in the face of an ever-more-interwoven government, which increasingly drifted away from the modern administrative state that the consensus had helped create. Performance problems grew from this gap, and those performance problems in turn fed the gridlock that increasingly crippled American democracy. It is impossible not to marvel at the remarkable foundation built by the Progressives—from both the Republican and Democratic parties—over more than a century. They proved it was possible to fight over what government should do but to find common ground in building the capacity to do it well. We have not lost the taste for fighting about what government should do. We have lost the shared commitment about the positive role that government can—indeed, must—play in the lives of citizens. We have also slipped from consensus on making government professional, effective, and accountable in doing its work, and that vastly complicates government's responsibility to deliver services to citizens.

We should never expect that we can sweep away partisan differences—or that we ought to try. Rough-and-tumble politics have characterized governments as long as humans have built governments. The healthiest piece of democracy is its ability to structure and resolve conflict. But we certainly could expect that government could regain its commitment to doing well what it chooses to do. It would be the basis of a more honest conversation between elected officials and citizens, it would help steer around the political quicksand that too often devours our leaders, and it would at least avoid making the problem of distrust in government even worse. Those relatively small steps could have a big impact on the American civic life.

NEW GOVERNANCE FOR NEW PROBLEMS

The challenge of adapting government to shifting problems is both ageless and universal. Consider this wise observation: "As the circumstances and challenges we face continue to change, we become less capable of responding to their demands. If we do not improve our professional level at every opportunity, over time we will lose the ability to fulfill the arduous tasks of leadership in reform." The words are from China's general secretary, Xi Jinping, in 2013.[2] The biggest challenge of governance, across the globe, is adapting the institutions and processes of government to the new problems it faces, without cutting the cords that tie it to the nation's enduring values. When

Americans tackled this challenge, they built on the bipartisan Progressive consensus that government could be made more professional, more effective, and more robust, all without making it less accountable or more tyrannical. The great challenge for the 21st century is maintaining the fundamental values of American government—a commitment to a government that does what citizens want without trampling excessively on their freedoms—while improving its ability to perform. Chinese leaders certainly understand the need to adapt. Americans deserve no less, all the more because America's cherished freedoms depend on it in ways that Chinese citizens could scarcely imagine.

As the Progressive movement was taking place in the early 20th century, many of its stalwarts, like Theodore Roosevelt and Wisconsin's "Fighting Bob" La Follette, cut their political teeth as Republicans. The Progressive Party celebrated its short political life in its 1912 platform by emphatically stating, "Political parties exist to secure responsible government and to execute the will of the people," instead of the "corrupt interests which use them impartially to serve their selfish purposes."[3] The theme resonates across the decades. Indeed, many Americans—and even some of their leaders—have lost faith in government's ability to be responsible, to execute the law well, and to serve all the people instead of narrow special interests. In the Progressive spirit is an echo of Hamilton and the nation's founders: Government that serves the people well is one of the most important blessings of civilization.

The founders surely would be aghast at the erosion of the commitment to competence. A government ill executed is surely bad government. Even worse is an ill-executed government that becomes, in turn, a pillar of gridlock.

But it does not have to be that way. This book has three lessons. One is that the outlines of a new strategy of governance have already begun to take shape, through strategies to manage interwoven government through effective use of evidence and data. The second is that we do not have to take this on faith. Skilled leaders, both inside the government and out, have already demonstrated how to make this work. The third is that successful government is possible, even amid the turbulence of the 21st century, if government's leaders have the instinct to lead, especially by building a strong public service and by using strong information systems as the central nervous system of an increasingly interwoven government.

On the other hand, the fuse on even bigger problems has been lit. We are pushing more programs out of government into a system of proxies that too often fail and are not held accountable. The fuse is burning quickly and is likely to hit the detonator of even larger headaches of governance and politics. That will not be good politics, policy, or democracy. And, given the interconnectedness of everything, it will not be good for the rest of the world either.

REWEAVING THE FABRIC

In chapter 7 I laid out four scenarios about how American government might evolve in the 21st century:

—*Weakened government*, in which government relies relatively less on evidence and has relatively less interweaving of government work in nongovernmental hands.

—*Musclebound government*, in which government relies relatively less on evidence but shares more of its work with the nongovernmental world.

—*Empowered government*, in which government relies relatively more on evidence but has less interweaving.

—*Leveraged government*, in which government relies more on evidence in managing an even more interwoven world of governance.

Where does America's future lie? We could answer by predicting what is most likely to happen. Another answer could build on hope: What scenario is most likely to advance the cause of American democracy for the century?

Consider first the case for greater use of information and evidence. In a fascinating paper, Archon Fong makes the case for greater transparency and use of information, in what he calls "infotopia." He says, "Information can be harnessed by democratic agents to reduce threats to citizens' vital interests" and makes an powerful case for government to do so. "Information is never sufficient to secure important democratic values," he points out, "but information about organizations upon which we depend is necessary for determining the extent to which those organizations advance or jeopardize our interests."[4] The volume of information available to both citizens and policymakers is surely not likely to diminish. The case for greater use of evidence is inescapable. As we saw in chapter 6, however, there are often significant barriers to effective use of evidence. But it surely is more desirable that government in the future will make greater use of evidence and information, for precisely the reasons that Fong suggests.

That pushes both the weakened and musclebound governments to the side, although a musclebound scenario is surely possible if the trends toward interweaving continue and if the search for better information shifts to a use of information to deflect political attack and to demonstrate compliance. In fact, powerful forces constantly construct barriers to the kind of transparency that Fong recommends and, because every bit of useful information has political meaning, the chances are great that the fight for greater transparency and use of evidence will become embroiled in short-term tactical battles and long-term strategic campaigns. But Fong is realistic. "Infotopia would not achieve Utopia," he concludes.[5] The scenarios stake out the edges of the playing field, and it is unlikely the future will fit squarely in any one of them. Given the enormous flood of information and the demands to improve government's capacity to deliver, it is a challenge to imagine a future that does not make significantly greater use of evidence. The weakened and musclebound scenarios are relatively unlikely and surely less desirable.

For all the reasons we explored in chapter 6, bringing more evidence into government is a difficult proposition. All evidence is gamed, and there are substantial organizational, analytical, and political barriers to using it effectively. In the case of Bode Technology's remarkable identification of the World Trade Center victims, however, there is an invaluable clue. The effective use of evidence depends on finding the right balance between supply forces (those who produce the information) and demand forces (those who use it). Government officials employ evidence when it is useful. When more evidence would be useful, their demand grows. Producing a new equilibrium—more supply meeting higher demands—will happen if those who supply evidence pay far more attention to producing evidence on the issues at play, in a form that policymakers will find most digestible, in ways that persuade. Supply will become more attuned to the needs of policymakers if those who analyze programs see that their work becomes incorporated into policy judgments. This, in turn, requires bridge building—in organizational, political, and analytical ways—between randomized controlled trials (and other forms of sophisticated decision-focused analysis) and performance management (and other evidence on the *how* of policy execution). The barriers are substantial, but we have learned that the barriers can be crossed.[6]

The far more difficult proposition is both predicting the course of government's interweaving of its work with the nongovernmental world and managing that interweaving well. Chapter 2 argued that government's size was not likely to diminish, because demographic imperatives and citizens' demands are not going to decline. Budgetary constraints will make it difficult for government to grow. So the most probable size of government will be about what it is now, as it has been for generations.

And how will its work be done? DiIulio makes the powerful case for pulling more of government's management back within government.

That, he contends, would be both cheaper and more effective. It would strengthen accountability by creating a clearer line of sight from those who make policy to those who carry it out. Policymakers certainly would have an easier time knowing who is supposed to do what if those in charge of carrying out their decisions were within the government, instead of scattered through a complex chain of implementation. In fact, DiIulio's prescription is for a refit of the original Progressive movement for the information age. It would seek to strengthen government's professionalism, enhance its power to get its work done better, and hold it more accountable by reinforcing the organizational boundaries around government action.

Indeed, this scenario would advance an empowered government, with a clearer definition of its responsibilities and a stronger capacity to carry it out, accompanied by a robust use of evidence to fit government to the information age. It would diminish the use of contracts, grants, and other proxy tools and substitute a more direct government role for those things that government chooses to do. On cost and effectiveness, the jury is out. As we saw in chapter 7, analysts battle over whether contracting out saves the government money and, if so, in what programs the potential cost savings are the greatest. Furthermore, advocates of contracting out contend that the use of private partners increases the government's flexibility, its ability to tap new sources of expertise when needed, and its ability to get badly needed external perspective. As one government insider jokingly put it, "If you are a fish in the bowl, you don't know when the water gets dirty." The greater clarity of government's roles and tools would echo the driving themes of the original Progressive movement. The greater use of evidence would help it recover its lost commitment to competence.

This embrace of the empowered government scenario, however, would also bring a stark wake-up call. Politicians and citizens alike would have to confront, far more directly than they have since World War II, the true size and scope of their government, the services they expect, and what it takes to deliver them. That would surely prove breathtaking. Rising government debt has allowed policymakers to hide the real cost of public programs. Growing reliance on interwoven government has allowed policymakers to hide the instruments of delivering those programs. Much of the political score-keeping of government's size has been by counts of the number of government employees. The Clinton administration's "reinventing government" movement, for example, calculated its impact on reducing government's size by its pledge to shrink the federal workforce. A Republican plan in early 2015 proposed to cut the number of federal employees through attrition by 10 percent by 2020 and to penalize agencies that hired more than one replacement for every three workers who departed.[7] (With half of the nation's air-traffic controllers eligible to retire in the mid-2010s, replacing just one-third of the controllers who leave would cripple most air-traffic control facilities and make a lot of airplane passengers angry.) The number of federal employees has become disconnected from the government's size and scope. Without enough employees with the right skills, government has struggled to deliver the services that citizens expect.

A frank conversation about what it would take to sync government's workforce with its responsibilities would be fascinating. That degree of directness, of course, would also require both Democrats and Republicans to confront the stark implications of the choices they have made since World War II. It would also lead them to conclusions that neither party could easily accept. Empowered government, with far more reliance on evidence and less interweaving, along with a stronger direct role for what government does, would surely clarify government's work and improve its operations. But it could prove a prospect too terrifying to take root.

A LEVERAGED FUTURE?

That leaves leveraged government on the table: a government that takes far greater advantage of evidence but operates in a world of even greater interweaving. This scenario might not offer the advantages of transparency and clarity of operations that would come from empowered government, but it does have one overwhelming advantage. It offers the potential for creating a remodeled approach to the Progressive commitment to competence without requiring either Republicans or Democrats to change the positions they have carefully honed for three generations. Leveraged government—more use of evidence and more interweaving—tracks most closely with the instincts of both parties, over the past two generations, when confronted with new problems. The Bush administration pursued social progress through partnerships with faith-based institutions. Its education program, No Child Left Behind, worked through local governments to increase standards and target schools with low-income students. When the Obama administration confronted the economic crisis in early 2009, its stimulus program pumped out more than $800 billion in stimulus money, mainly to individuals through the tax code and through infrastructure investments to state and local governments. Its health care program worked through tax incentives, tax penalties, employer mandates, and other proxy mechanisms. No matter how strong the small-government rhetoric, neither party can escape creating new initiatives to attack big problems. Neither party can escape citizens' demands to respond when crises loom. Their responses have become increasingly hardwired to work through interwoven strategies rather than running programs in-house. Leveraged government seems government's most likely future path.

This would be a different foundation for 21st-century governance from the one the Progressives laid more than a century ago. That tradition grew on a foundation that promoted government's power and recognized the need to hold it accountable. It foundered as it transitioned from clarity of purpose and structure to complexity and ambiguity through interwoven strategies. It is impossible, of course, to make government simpler. Indeed, an important strength of the evolving nature of interwoven governance is that it syncs with society's increasing complexity and with the growing interconnection of the public, private, nonprofit, national, and global perspectives on all things that matter. But it is surely possible that continuing down the current path will create a government whose capacity is increasingly out of sync with the demands placed on it, a government that increasingly fails to perform and is ever more unaccountable, and a government that continually reinforces citizens' distrust because it struggles to perform.

This need not be America's future. Among the programs GAO identified as the most prone to fraud, waste, and abuse, the managers of nearly two dozen of them proved they could conquer their problems. Bright new managers like Sofia Hussain prove that it is possible to conquer sophisticated twists to old challenges, like breaking the back of Ponzi schemes that rob grandmothers of their life savings, by employing cutting-edge technology to make government work better, faster. A leveraged government is not a prescription for mismanagement and poor democracy. But it is a road map to a government that is more complicated and more interwoven with the nongovernmental world, and it will take especially skillful government officials to navigate its pathways.

In fact, the program managers who have made their way off the high-risk list identify the path that successfully managing leveraged government requires. They chart the path to a commitment to competence, through four essential tools.

1. Performance metrics. Making progress requires tracking progress. The Moneyball movement has championed bringing more evidence to government. The performance-management movement has developed increasingly sophisticated techniques for measuring and motivating high-quality results. Championed first in the New York City Police Department, then expanded citywide in Baltimore, taken to the state level in Maryland, and used at the federal level in a remarkable partnership to reduce homelessness among veterans between the

Department of Housing and Urban Development and the Department of Veterans Affairs, performance management is a fundamental tool for measuring and encouraging progress. It is impossible to move performance forward without setting a direction and tracking how quickly a program is moving. Moreover, as more programs operate across agency, governmental, and national boundaries, tracking performance on important goals can become a language that tracks across these boundaries. In the information age, it can also provide a new backbone for accountability to replace the traditional one that the growing complexity of public programs has weakened. And in coping with the tough barriers that often hinder the use of better evidence, beginning with the basics—tracking what works best in delivering the services that citizens count on the most—it offers hope in finding the needed balance between the forces of information supply and demand.

2. Technology management. Better information and evidence, of course, requires better technology, in collecting, analyzing, and distributing what we learn. This is the underlying lesson of the "big data" movement: We can both gather more data and make even better use of the data we have. Government managers are tracking the location of crimes and the incidence of food-borne illnesses. They are extracting valuable lessons from local 311 systems and using remote-sensing satellites to gauge climate forces. As technology has become more important in driving data, however, it has become increasingly hard to manage. Government is often skating on the bleeding edge of technology and it invariably relies heavily on private contractors to design, build, and manage the systems. That combination has often produced big performance problems. It's ironic that the fundamental step to improve government's results has become enmeshed in the very problems it is trying to solve. So profound are the technology management problems, in fact, that GAO in 2015 placed the management of information technology on its high-risk list.[8] It is a challenge, as one government insider put it, like the intricate dance moves that Fred Astaire and Ginger Rogers popularized on-screen in the 1930s—except that the government is often playing the role of Rogers, dancing backward while wearing heels. It is an important and essential dance—and government usually has the harder steps.

3. Managing boundaries. The original Progressive movement grew in a bureaucratic world of firm boundaries. Drawing clear boundaries, in fact, was the way the Progressives reconciled their desire to increase bureaucratic power with the imperative to hold it accountable. With the growing complexity of government programs in the late 20th century, however, bureaucratic boundaries became less a strategy for ensuring effectiveness and accountability than a source of pathology. Boundaries became silos that restrained innovation and flexibility. Bureaucracies often evolved into loose holding companies of expertise, with more of their work taking place through proxies. Government leaders spent less time managing programs within their bureaucratic worlds and more orchestrating complex partnerships, often involving nongovernmental partners and almost always partners outside their own turf. The future belongs to the boundary spanners.

4. Human capital. All of these tools point in one singular direction: The increasing complexity of government programs, the need for stronger performance metrics and information technology, and the imperative for boundary spanners all require more smart government managers. As proxy tools have come to dominate government, each government manager leverages more money, as we saw in chapter 5, with workers in civilian programs leveraging eight times more money in 2010, on average, than they did in 1940. With roughly the same number of workers leveraging more money, the need for highly skilled government workers is growing exponentially.

Managing leveraged government is a tall order, but it is eminently doable. The agencies that got their programs off the high-risk list have demonstrated the game plan. More important, they have sketched the framework for a government with the capacity to deliver without creating a government that is overbearing or intrusive, a government that is accountable without struggling to stay within an outmoded accountability system constrained within boundaries, and a government that is smart because it is run by smart managers with information age tools. The government of the future is already here, if we have our wits about us to build on the lessons we have already learned.

DISRUPTERS

There is a chance, of course, that the future might not cooperate with the forces already in motion. One could imagine disrupters that could derail or undermine the movement toward the model of governance I have outlined.

1. Cyberthreats. The leveraged government model depends heavily on evidence and information technology, much of which is dependent on a robust and trustworthy Internet. For an untold number of interactions every day, from Facebook posts to Amazon purchases, that trust holds. But increasing breaches of this trust may mean it will be hard to maintain. In 2014 the North Korean government attacked Sony Pictures over a motion picture depicting a fictional attempt on the life of the country's president. Foreign e-criminals burrowed into the IRS accounts of 100,000 taxpayers in 2015 to obtain fraudulent refunds; hackers made off with the personnel data of 4.2 million current and former federal workers; and the VA fought off a billion hackers a month seeking to get access to its computer systems. The Internet was built to be an open network, allowing anyone to connect with anyone else. "It's not that we didn't think about security," MIT computer scientist David D. Clark told the *Washington Post*. "We knew that there were untrustworthy people out there, and we thought we could exclude them." Of course, they guessed wrong. Google vice president Vinton G. Cerf, who designed some of the Internet's key elements, reminded critics that the system's designers had their hands full simply getting it up and running. "We didn't focus on how you could wreck this system intentionally."[9] But it has become clear that it is quite possible to do so. A major attack in the future could increase users' fears that their financial security and personal privacy could be damaged by too much information interconnection. Already signs have emerged that the WikiLeaks disclosures of information collected by the National Security Agency have made some consumers gun-shy about e-connections. It is possible that a large-scale breach could increase the wariness of citizens—and their government—about the Internet. There is no going back to pen and paper, but the pace of future reliance on information technology could be significantly affected by fears about information security.

2. New technologies. On the other hand, new technologies could create unexpected changes in the way citizens and governments use information. The managers at BlackBerry never expected that Apple's upstart product, without a physical keyboard, could wipe out their business model—and their business. Taxi drivers never imagined that the Internet could create a network for riders to connect with drivers and threaten their livelihood. Smartphone apps that allow drivers to pay for parking before meters expire have dramatically cut parking ticket revenue—in Washington, D.C., in 2013, by almost 7 percent. Other apps keep drivers posted on the location of enforcement stations (that is, speed traps) and can also reduce income from tickets. Given the purchasing cycles of much government information technology, most of the hardware that governments will use in the near term is already in place. When Microsoft announced in 2014 that it was ending its free support for Windows XP, the federal government scrambled to figure out how best to keep security patched for hundreds of thousands of computers still using the operating system 13 years after release, including many processing classified data.[10] On one hand, there is a large and growing sunk cost in existing technologies that are hard to uproot. On the other hand, it is possible that major technological breakthroughs could quickly change everything.

3. National security threats. The strong trend since World War II has been to interweave more of government's operations with the private sector. But it is possible that a major national security crisis could lead to calls for a big expansion in government's role—and for having more of that role managed by government itself, and by government's own employees. That was precisely what happened after the September 11 terrorist attacks, when Congress and the Bush administration created a massive new cabinet department, the Department of Homeland Security, and transformed airport security workers from private contractors to government employees. In just weeks, a new agency with more than 54,000 federal employees took shape. Government's interweaving of its role with nongovernmental partners is strong and powerful, but it is not inevitable. National security threats could pull some of government's power back to within government while interweaving expands in other areas.

4. Economic crisis. Finally, economic crisis could disrupt the long-term trends in the size and patterns of American government. Large-scale unemployment and fundamental economic insecurity could transform the way that Americans and their policymakers look at government—and create big demands for cutting government down. Such insecurity could also increase the demand for more protection by government against economic threats and uncertainty. Of course, we have had a taste of how American government might respond to an enormous economic event, with the Great Recession that began in 2008. The threat was huge, grew rapidly, and quickly outstripped conventional approaches to economic management. The government launched a powerful response aimed at preventing the bad from getting worse. And it is worth pointing out that almost all the tools it used involved a rapid increase in interweaving, from federal grants to state and local governments, bailouts for the auto and financial industries, tougher regulations, and cross-boundary coordination between agencies like the Treasury and Federal Reserve that had often guarded their operating independence.

Thus, it is certainly possible to imagine disrupters that would twist or even deflect the path that makes leveraged government the most likely path for America's future. Moreover, there are other disrupters that seem unimaginable—or that have not been imagined—that could have an even more profound effect. Weighing all these forces in the balance, however, the best bet is that the road from the present to America in 2030 and beyond is likely to be that of leveraged government. It is a future for which America's current patterns of governance are increasingly out of sync. It is a future for which we need a new commitment to competence, built on a fresh model. It is a future for which, fortunately, we have elements in place on which we can build. And it is a future we will surely regret if we do not.

REBUILDING THE COMMITMENT TO COMPETENCE

The original Progressive spirit was not devoted to building *big* government. Neither was it a tool of liberal Democrats. It was a remarkably bipartisan strategy with a singular goal: building a *good* government, one that worked. Politics was not any less rugged in those days of the late 1880s. There were fierce battles to break the trusts and to position America as a genuine world power. The two dominant political parties fractured and government's fundamental role was at the core of the debate. But amid this fierce turmoil, the parties created a consensus—sometimes uneasy, always fluid—that what government chose to do, it had an obligation to do well. As the original Progressive movement slowly disintegrated, that consensus eroded, too. It is hard to reject the proposition, however, that there are many things that almost everyone thinks government needs to do and, having taken on these jobs, it needs to do them well. It is difficult to conceive how American government can survive even the middle of the 21st century and stay true to the vision of its founders if it fails to serve the expectations of its citizens, no matter how tough the underlying battles about those expectations might be.

It would be folly to think that this straightforward proposition could sweep away the gridlock that has seized up the political system. But it is possible to imagine that the warring political parties could at least grudgingly agree that poor performance is not good for the economy, not good for citizens' trust in the job they do, and not good for their own political future. Big performance problems have increasingly become dangerous politics, as both George W. Bush and Barack Obama came, too late, to discover. There is reason enough to build a renewed commitment to serving citizens and, ultimately, the public interest well. But there is an even more practical reason to build a new commitment to competence. The failure to do so will prove politically punishing for elected officials who fail to deliver—and fail they will if they try to use outmoded techniques on new problems. That could prove a powerful political case for embracing the renewed commitment to competence, and a stark warning for politicians who do not.

We could do it the easy way, with political opponents choosing to shift the fight to the *what* of public policy while agreeing that citizens deserve expert execution of the *how* of policy. That, of course, was the base on which the Progressives of both parties built the modern American state and advanced it for more than a century. That might not be likely, however. The political disputes are so intense that the warring parties might want to seize any chance to continue each battle on every possible front. And that is a prescription for even more gridlock.

That means that we might need to do it the hard way, with big crises and nagging worries about government performance finally forcing government to deliver on what it promises. Bigger problems are certain unless we build the government we need for the problems we must solve. In fact, the pace of problems will accelerate unless we deal effectively with the ones already before us. When we do decide, the road map is there, in smarter human capital, better evidence, and an effective bridge-building strategy for interwoven gridlock. That is the key to unlocking gridlock, at least in the execution of government's most important programs.

Of course, elected officials could ignore the opportunity and remain trapped, by intention or accident, in an ever-deepening chasm of government performance problems. If American government ultimately fails, it will be because its 18th-century institutions cannot cope with a 21st-century world. But I am both an optimist and a realist. The realist in me recognizes that elected officials will continue to use sharp elbows on tough problems within contentious politics. After all, the floor of Independence Hall was not a quiet place as the founders debated independence and the new Constitution. But the optimist in me believes that elected officials, looking out for the good of their constituents and for the country, as well as their own political hides, will at some point not tolerate a government that fails to perform. The key lies in the fundamentals of recovering America's lost commitment to competence.

Notes

PREFACE

1. Francis Fukuyama, *Political Order and Political Decay: From the Industrial Revolution to the Globalization of Democracy* (New York: Farrar, Straus and Giroux, 2014).

2. Thomas E. Mann and Norman J. Ornstein, *It's Even Worse than It Looks: How the American Constitutional System Collided with the New Politics of Extremism* (New York: Basic Books, 2012).

CHAPTER ONE

1. Interview with the author, May 21, 2015.

2. Quinnipiac University National Poll, August 31, 2015 (www.quinnipiac .edu/news-and-events/quinnipiac-university-poll/national/release-detail ?ReleaseID=2275).

3. Global Strategy Group, "GSGCompass," 2015 (http://globalstrategy group.com/wp-content/uploads/2015/09/GSG-Compass_Sept-2015 _Smaller-Isnt-Better.pdf?wpmm=1&wpisrc=nl_daily202).

4. Harper Lee, *Go Set a Watchman* (New York: HarperCollins, 2015), p. 198.

5. Ronald Reagan, news conference, August 12, 1986 (www.reagan foundation.org/reagan-quotes-detail.aspx?tx=2079).

6. John J. DiIulio Jr., *Bring Back the Bureaucrats* (West Conshohocken, Pa.: Templeton Press, 2014).

7. James Madison, speech at the Virginia Ratifying Convention, June 20, 1788.

8. John F. Kennedy, "Remarks to Members of the White House Conference on National Economic Issues," May 21, 1962 (www.presidency.ucsb.edu /ws/?pid=8670).

9. Tom Harbour, statement before the Subcommittee on Oversight, Investigations, and Management, Committee on Homeland Security, U.S. House of Representatives, October 17, 2011 (https://docs.google.com/viewer ?url=http%3A%2F%2Fhomeland.house.gov%2Fsites%2Fhomeland.house .gov%2Ffiles%2FTestimony%2520Harbour.pdf).

10. Ross Ramsay, "Federal Government Is Very Unpopular with Texas Voters," *Texas Tribune*, February 26, 2015 (www.texastribune.org/2015/02/26 /uttt-poll-least-popular-government/).

11. FAA press release, "Airline Passenger Travel to Nearly Double in Two Decades," March 8, 2012 (www.faa.gov/news/press_releases/news_story.cfm ?newsId=13394).

12. U.S. GAO, "Mitigating Gaps in Weather Satellite Data," February 11, 2015 (www.gao.gov/highrisk/mitigating_gaps_in_weather_satellite_data /why_did_study#t=0).

13. U.S. GAO, "Government-Wide Estimates and Use of Death Data to Help Prevent Payments to Deceased Individuals" (www.gao.gov/products /GAO-15-482T).

14. Defense One, "VA Blocked More Than a Billion Cyber Threats in March," May 3, 2015 (www.defenseone.com/technology/2015/05/va-blocked -billions-cyber-threats-march/111721/).

15. FHWA, "Deficient Bridges by State and Highway System 2014," December 2014 (www.fhwa.dot.gov/bridge/nbi/no10/defbr14.cfm).

CHAPTER TWO

1. Organization for Economic Cooperation and Development, *Government at a Glance: 2014* (Paris: OECD, 2014) (http://dx.doi.org/10.1787/888932942241).

2. U.S. Office of Personnel Management, *Federal Employment Reports: December 2012*, table 9 (www.opm.gov/policy-data-oversight/data-analysis-documentation/federal-employment-reports/employment-trends-data/2012/december/table-9/).

3. Organization for Economic Cooperation and Development, *Government at a Glance: 2013* (Paris: OECD, 2013), figure 3.22 (http://dx.doi.org/10.1787/888932941709).

4. Ibid., figure 3.23 (http://dx.doi.org/10.1787/888932941728).

5. Ezra Klein, "The U.S. Government: An Insurance Conglomerate Protected by a Large, Standing Army," *Washington Post*, February 14, 2011 (http://voices.washingtonpost.com/ezra-klein/2011/02/the_us_government_an_insurance.html).

6. Congressional Budget Office, *An Update to the Budget and Economic Outlook: 2014 to 2024* (Washington, D.C., August 2014), table 4 (www.cbo.gov/publication/45249).

7. Congressional Budget Office, *The Budget and Economic Outlook: 2015 to 2025* (Washington: CBO, 2015) (www.cbo.gov/publication/49892).

8. Congressional Budget Office, *An Update*, p. 21.

9. U.S. Government Accountability Office, *State and Local Governments' Fiscal Outlook: 2014 Update*, GAO-15-224SP (2014) (www.gao.gov/assets/670/667623.pdf).

10. Bianca DiJulio, Jamie Firth, and Mollyann Brodie, "Data Note: Americans' Views on the U.S. Role in Global Health," Henry J. Kaiser Foundation, January 23, 2015 (http://kff.org/global-health-policy/poll-finding/data-note-americans-views-on-the-u-s-role-in-global-health/).

11. WorldPublicOpinion.org, "American Public Opinion on Foreign Aid," November 30, 2010 (www.worldpublicopinion.org/pipa/pdf/nov10/ForeignAid_Nov10_quaire.pdf).

12. Sustainable Governance Indicators, "To What Extent Are Citizens Informed of Government Policymaking?" (www.sgi-network.org/2014/Gover

nance/Executive_Accountability/Citizens%E2%80%99_Participatory
_Competence/Policy_Knowledge).

13. "How Ignorant Are Americans?" Newsweek.com, March 20, 2011
(www.newsweek.com/how-ignorant-are-americans-66053).

CHAPTER THREE

1. The case comes from U.S. Centers for Disease Control and Prevention, "Outbreak of Salmonella Serotype Saintpaul Infections Associated with
Multiple Raw Produce Items—United States, 2008," August 29, 2008 (www
.cdc.gov/mmwr/preview/mmwrhtml/mm5734a1.htm).

2. U.S. Centers for Disease Control and Prevention, "CDC Estimates
of Foodborne Illness in the United States," April 17, 2014 (www.cdc.gov
/foodborneburden/estimates-overview.html).

3. Brady Denis, "FDA Unveils Rules to Make Imported Food Meet
U.S. Standards," *Washington Post*, July 26, 2013 (www.washingtonpost.com
/national/health-science/fda-unveils-rules-to-make-imported-food-meet
-us-standards/2013/07/26/659d4bf0-f4b0-11e2-aa2e-4088616498b4_story
.html).

4. U.S. Government Accountability Office, *Food Safety: Additional Actions
Needed to Help FDA's Foreign Offices Ensure Safety of Imported Food*, GAO-15-
183, January 2015, p. 13 (www.gao.gov/assets/670/668230.pdf).

5. John Kamensky, "National Partnership for Reinventing Government:
A Brief History," January 1999 (http://govinfo.library.unt.edu/npr/whoweare
/history2.html).

6. OPM; and Kaiser Family Foundation, "Workers by Occupational
Category," 2013 (http://kff.org/other/state-indicator/blue-and-white-collar
-workers/).

7. Oceana, "Oceana Reveals Chronic Mislabeling of Iconic Chesapeake
Bay Blue Crab," 2015 (http://usa.oceana.org/sites/default/files/oceana_crab
_report_medrez.pdf).

8. Lisa Rein, "In Dallas, the IRS Says It Can't Chase Tax Cheats Who
Owe Less Than $1 Million," WashingtonPost.com, April 8, 2015 (www
.washingtonpost.com/blogs/federal-eye/wp/2015/04/08/in-dallas-the-irs

-says-it-cant-chase-tax-cheats-who-owe-less-than-1-million/?tid
=hpModule_14fd66a0-9199-11e2-bdea-e32ad90da239&hpid=z14).

9. David B. Caruso, "VA Makes Little Headway in Fight to Shorten
Waits for Care," MilitaryTimes.com, April 9, 2015 (www.militarytimes.com
/story/military/benefits/veterans/2015/04/09/va-wait-times-continue
/25422103/).

10. Kathleen Day, "Taxpayers Own a Whole Town Because of an S&L's
Failure," LosAngelesTimes.com, July 12, 1989 (http://articles.latimes.com
/1989-07-12/business/fi-3600_1_federal-government).

11. U.S. Office of Management and Budget, *Budget of the United States Government, Fiscal Year 2016: Analytical Perspectives*, 2015, p. 77 (www.whitehouse
.gov/sites/default/files/omb/budget/fy2016/assets/ap_8_strengthening
.pdf).

12. Terry W. Culler, "Most Federal Workers Need Only Be Competent,"
Wall Street Journal, May 21, 1986, p. 32.

13. OMB, *Analytical Perspectives, Budget of the United States Government,
Fiscal Year 2016*, p. 86.

14. Ibid., p. 82.

15. Ibid.

16. Among others, see Donald F. Kettl, Constance Horner, Patricia W.
Ingraham, and Ronald P. Sanders, *Civil Service Reform: Building a Govern-
ment That Works* (Washington, D.C.: Brookings Institution Press, 1996); and
Partnership for Public Service, *Building the Enterprise: A New Civil Service
Framework*, 2014 (http://ourpublicservice.org/publications/viewcontent
details.php?id=18).

17. Janet V. Denhardt and Robert B. Denhardt, *The New Public Service:
Serving, Not Steering*, 3rd ed. (New York: Routledge, 2011).

CHAPTER FOUR

1. Brad Plumer, "How the U.S. Manages to Waste $165 Billion in Food
Each Year," WashingtonPost.com, August 22, 2012 (www.washingtonpost
.com/blogs/wonkblog/wp/2012/08/22/how-food-actually-gets-wasted-in
-the-united-states/).

2. U.S. Federal Aviation Administration, *Fiscal Year 2014 Summary of Performance and Financial Information*, 2014 (www.faa.gov/about/plans_reports /media/2014-FAA-PAR-Summary.pdf).

3. U.S. National Highway Traffic Safety Administration, "Fatal Crashes 1994–2013" (www-fars.nhtsa.dot.gov/Trends/TrendsGeneral.aspx).

4. U.S. Environmental Protection Agency, "Air Quality Trends" (www .epa.gov/airtrends/aqtrends.html).

5. U.S. Fire Administration, "U.S. Fire Statistics" (www.usfa.fema.gov /data/statistics/#tabs2).

6. Patrick Henry, March 23, 1775 (http://avalon.law.yale.edu/18th _century/patrick.asp).

7. See Donald F. Kettl, *Government by Proxy: (Mis?)Managing Federal Programs* (Washington, D.C.: CQ Press, 1988). See also Lester M. Salamon, "Rethinking Public Management: Third-Party Government and the Changing Forms of Government Action," *Public Policy* 29 (1981), pp. 259–78; Lester M. Salamon, ed., *The Tools of Government: A Guide to the New Governance* (Oxford University Press, 2002); Frederick C. Mosher, "The Changing Responsibilities and Tactics of the Federal Government," in *American Public Administration: Patterns of the Past*, edited by James W. Fesler (Washington, D.C.: American Society for Public Administration, 1982), pp. 198–212; and H. Brinton Milward and Keith G. Provan, "Governing the Hollow State," *Journal of Public Administration Research and Theory* 10 (2000), pp. 359–80.

8. See, among others, Jacob A. Riis, *How the Other Half Lives: Studies among the Tenements of New York* (1890; reprint, New York: Garrett Press, 1970); Upton Sinclair, *The Jungle* (1906; reprint, Cambridge, Mass.: R. Bentley, 1971); Ida Tarbell, *The History of the Standard Oil Company* (1904; reprint, New York: Norton, 1966).

9. Quoted in Lloyd Milton Short, *The Development of National Administrative Organization in the United States* (Johns Hopkins University Press, 1923), p. 440.

10. Woodrow Wilson, "The Study of Administration," *Political Science Quarterly* 2 (1887), p. 220.

11. Office of Management and Budget, *Budget of the United States Government: Fiscal Year 2016—Historical Tables*, 2015, table 6-1 (www.whitehouse .gov/omb/budget/Historicals).

12. "Booz Allen Hamilton in Spotlight over Leak," CNNMoney, June 10, 2013 (http://money.cnn.com/2013/06/10/news/booz-allen-hamilton-leak/index.html).

13. Sarah L. Pettijohn and Elizabeth T. Boris with Carol J. De Vita and Saunji D. Fyffe, *Nonprofit-Government Contracts and Grants: Findings from the 2013 National Survey* (Washington, D.C.: Urban Institute, 2013) (www.urban.org/UploadedPDF/412962-Nonprofit-Government-Contracts-and-Grants.pdf), p. 4.

14. U.S. Bureau of the Census, *Statistical Abstract of the United States: 2012*, table 431 (https://docs.google.com/viewer?url=http%3A%2F%2Fwww.census.gov%2Fcompendia%2Fstatab%2F2012%2Ftables%2F12s0431.pdf).

15. "Remarks by the President in State of Union Address," January 25, 2011 (www.whitehouse.gov/the-press-office/2011/01/25/remarks-president-state-union-address).

16. Angie Drobnic Holan, "Obama Says the One Department Regulates Salmon in Freshwater and Another Regulates Them in Saltwater," *PolitiFact, Tampa Bay Times*, January 26, 2011 (www.politifact.com/truth-o-meter/statements/2011/jan/26/barack-obama/obama-says-one-department-regulates-salmon-freshwa/).

17. Nina Bernstein, "With Medicaid, Long-Term Care of Elderly Looms as a Rising Cost," NewYorkTimes.com, September 6, 2012 (www.nytimes.com/2012/09/07/health/policy/long-term-care-looms-as-rising-medicaid-cost.html?_r=0; and Henry J. Kaiser Family Foundation, "Overview of Nursing Facility Capacity, Financing, and Ownership in the United States in 2011," June 28, 2013 (http://kff.org/medicaid/fact-sheet/overview-of-nursing-facility-capacity-financing-and-ownership-in-the-united-states-in-2011/).

18. Martha Derthick, *Keeping the Compound Republic: Essays on American Federalism* (Brookings, 2001), p. 63.

19. For a powerful examination of the interlocking issues of the role of the state, the rule of law, and democracy, see Francis Fukuyama, *Political Order and Political Decay: From the Industrial Revolution to the Globalization of Democracy* (New York: Farrar, Straus, and Giroux, 2014).

20. John M. Gaus, "The Responsibility of Public Administration," in *The Frontiers of Public Administration*, edited by John M. Gaus, Leonard D. White, and Marshall E. Dimock (University of Chicago Press, 1936), p. 37.

21. Jody Freeman, "Extending Public Law Norms through Privatization," *Harvard Law Review* 116 (2003), pp. 1285–1352.

CHAPTER FIVE

1. "The Storm after the Storm," *60 Minutes*, March 1, 2015 (www.cbsnews .com/news/hurricane-sandy-60-minutes-fraud-investigation/).

2. Federal Emergency Management Agency, *Hurricane Sandy National Flood Insurance Program Claims Review*, 2015 (www.fema.gov/hurricane-sandy -national-flood-insurance-program-claims-review).

3. National Flood Insurance Program, "About the National Flood Insurance Program: The NFIP Partnership," 2015 (www.floodsmart.gov/flood smart/pages/about/nfip_partnership.jsp); and "About the National Flood Insurance Program: Coverage from the NFIP" (www.floodsmart.gov/flood smart/pages/about/coverage_from_nfip.jsp).

4. Eric Garcia, "What Brownie Regrets," *National Journal*, August 28, 2015 (www.nationaljournal.com/white-house/2015/08/28/what-michael -brown-regrets).

5. U.S. Government Accountability Office, *Improper Payments: Government-Wide Estimates and Use of Death Data to Help Prevent Payments to Deceased Individuals*, GAO-15-482T, March 16, 2015 (www.gao.gov/products/GAO -15-482T).

6. U.S. Office of Management and Budget, *Budget of the United States Government: Fiscal Year 2016*, table 25-12 (www.whitehouse.gov/sites/default /files/omb/budget/fy2016/assets/25_12.pdf).

7. Pew Research Center, "Trust in Government Nears Record Low, but Most Federal Agencies Are Viewed Favorably," October 18, 2013 (www .people-press.org/2013/10/18/trust-in-government-nears-record-low-but -most-federal-agencies-are-viewed-favorably/).

8. Bruce Bartlett, "Tax Cuts and 'Starving the Beast,'" May 7, 2010 (www .forbes.com/2010/05/06/tax-cuts-republicans-starve-the-beast-columnists -bruce-bartlett.html).

9. Deroy Murdock, "How to Defund Obamacare," *National Review*, August 30, 2013 (www.nationalreview.com/article/357218/how-defund-obama care-deroy-murdock).

10. U.S. Government Accountability Office, *Healthcare.gov: Contract Planning and Oversight Practices Were Ineffective Given the Challenges and Risks*, GAO-14-824T (http://docs.house.gov/meetings/IF/IF02/20140731 /102587/HHRG-113-IF02-Wstate-WoodsW-20140731.pdf).

11. Maya Nye, "Chemical Spill in West Virginia Offers Opportunity to Learn About and Improve Chemical Safety in America," April 15, 2014 (http://blog.epa.gov/ej/2014/04/another-chemical-spill/).

12. National Public Radio, "How Industrial Chemical Regulation Failed West Virginia," January 29, 2014 (www.npr.org/2014/01/29/268201454/how -industrial-chemical-regulation-failed-west-virginia).

13. Ibid.

14. Elizabeth Shogren, "Drinking Water Not Tested for Tens of Thousands of Chemicals," National Public Radio, January 24, 2014 (www.npr.org /blogs/thesalt/2014/01/24/265520673/drinking-water-not-tested-for-tens -of-thousands-of-chemicals).

15. "Biggest IRS Scam Around: Identity Tax Refund Fraud," *60 Minutes*, September 21, 2014 (www.cbsnews.com/news/irs-scam-identity-tax-refund -fraud-60-minutes/).

16. U.S. Government Accountability Office, *Identity Theft: Additional Actions Could Help IRS Combat the Large, Evolving Threat of Refund Fraud*, GAO-14-633, August 2014 (www.gao.gov/assets/670/665368.pdf).

17. Gallup, "Record High in U.S. Say Big Government Greatest Threat," December 18, 2013 (www.gallup.com/poll/166535/record-high-say-big -government-greatest-threat.aspx).

18. Rasmussen Reports, "37% of Voters Fear the Federal Government," April 18, 2014 (www.rasmussenreports.com/public_content/politics /general_politics/april_2014/37_of_voters_fear_the_federal_govern ment).

19. Pew Research Center for People and the Press, "Anger, Frustration with the Federal Government," December 18, 2013 (www.people-press.org /2013/10/18/trust-in-government-nears-record-low-but-most-federal -agencies-are-viewed-favorably/10-18-13-6/).

20. OECD, *Government at a Glance: 2013* (Paris: OECD, 2013), p. 33 (www.oecd.org/gov/govataglance.htm).

21. Ibid., pp. 33–34.

22. Geert Bouckaert and Steven Van de Walle, "Comparing Measures of Citizen Trust and User Satisfaction as Indicators of 'Good Governance': Difficulties in Linking Trust and Satisfaction Indicators," *International Review of Administrative Sciences* 69 (2013), pp. 329–43.

23. Russell Hardin, "Government without Trust," *Journal of Trust Research* 3 (2003), pp. 32, 48.

Chapter Six

1. Jim Nussle and Peter Orszag, *Moneyball for Government* (Washington, D.C.: Disruption Books, 2014), p. 4.

2. Charles E. Lindblom and David K. Cohen, *Usable Knowledge: Social Science and Social Problem Solving* (Yale University Press, 1979), p. 12.

3. Public Policy Polling, "Conspiracy Theory Poll Results," April 2, 2013 (www.publicpolicypolling.com/main/2013/04/conspiracy-theory-poll-results-.html).

4. Finding Bigfoot (www.animalplanet.com/tv-shows/finding-bigfoot/videos/northern-new-jersey-has-a-mysterious-history-with-bigfoot-sightings/).

5. International Association of Fire Chiefs, "You Can't Help . . . If You Don't Arrive" (www.iafc.org/files/1SAFEhealthSHS/VehclSafety_IAFC posterBW.pdf).

6. Massimo Calabresi, "CIA Chief: Pakistan Would Have Jeopardized bin Laden," *Time*, May 2, 2011 (http://swampland.time.com/2011/05/03/cia-chief-breaks-silence-u-s-ruled-out-involving-pakistan-in-bin-laden-raid-early-on/).

7. Robert Siegel, "In Facing National Security Dilemmas, CIA Puts Probabilities into Words," *National Public Radio*, July 23, 2014 (www.npr.org/2014/07/23/334494673/in-facing-national-security-dilemmas-cia-puts-probabilities-into-words).

8. Craig Whitlock and Barton Gellman, "To Hunt Osama bin Laden, Satellites Watched over Abbottabad, Pakistan, and Navy SEALs," *Washington Post*, August 29, 2013 (www.washingtonpost.com/world/national-security/to-hunt-osama-bin-laden-satellites-watched-over-abbottabad-pakistan-and-navy-seals/2013/08/29/8d32c1d6-10d5-11e3-b4cb-fd7ce041d814_story.html).

9. Richard Wray, "Internet Data Heads for 500bn Gigabytes," *Guardian*, May 18, 2009 (www.theguardian.com/business/2009/may/18/digital-content -expansion).

10. MG Siegler, "Eric Schmidt: Every 2 Days We Create as Much Information as We Did Up to 2003," TechCrunch.com, August 4, 2010 (http:// techcrunch.com/2010/08/04/schmidt-data/).

11. SINTEF (Scandinavia), "Big Data, for Better or Worse: 90% of World's Data Generated over Last Two Years," *Science Daily*, May 22, 2013 (www.sciencedaily.com/releases/2013/05/130522085217.htm).

12. Office of Management and Budget, "Strengthening the Federal Workforce," *Budget of the United States Government: Fiscal 2016—Analytical Perspectives*, 2015, p. 86 (www.whitehouse.gov/sites/default/files/omb/budget /fy2016/assets/ap_8_strengthening.pdf).

13. Irving L. Janis, *Victims of Groupthink: A Psychological Study of Foreign-Policy Decisions and Fiascoes* (Boston: Houghton, Mifflin, 1972); Cass R. Sunstein and Reid Hastie, *Wiser: Getting beyond Groupthink to Make Groups Smarter* (Boston: Harvard Business Review Press, 2015).

14. Cass R. Sunstein and Reid Hastie, " 'Happy Talk' and the Dangers of Groupthink," *Time*, January 14, 2015 (http://time.com/3668083/happy-talk -groupthink-leadership/).

15. Charles E. Lindblom, "The Science of 'Muddling Through,' " *Public Administration Review* 19 (1959), pp. 79–88; James G. March and Herbert A. Simon, *Organizations* (New York: Wiley, 1958), pp. 140–41.

16. Alice Rivlin, *Systematic Thinking for Social Action* (Brookings, 1971), pp. 2–5.

17. This was precisely what Lindblom and Cohen found in 1979.

18. National Institute of Standards, "National Institute of Standards and Technology Federal Building and Fire Safety Investigation of the World Trade Center Disaster," August 30, 2006 (www.nist.gov/public_affairs /factsheet/wtc_faqs_082006.cfm); Jeffrey W. Vincoli, Norman H. Black, and Stewart C. Burkhammer, "SH&E at Ground Zero: Professional Response," *Professional Safety* (May 2002), p. 27 (web.archive.org/web/20030623013242 /http://www.asse.org/ps0502vincoli.pdf). For the background cite on deaths, please see http://911research.wtc7.net/wtc/evidence/bodies.html.

19. Thomas Bode, interview with the author, July 18, 2014.

20. Stephanie Stoiloff, Paul Ferrara, and Randy Nagy, "Working Together to Solve Crime," *Forensic Magazine*, February 1, 2010 (www.forensicmag.com /articles/2010/02/working-together-solve-crime); Vesna Jaksic, "DNA Databases May Be Growing Too Quickly," *National Law Journal*, January 12, 2007 (www.nationallawjournal.com/id=900005471454/DNA-databases-may-be -growing-too-quickly?slreturn=20140704153330).

21. Robert Lee Hotz, "Probing the DNA of Death," *Los Angeles Times*, October 9, 2002 (www.jonhoyle.com/GeneCodes/LATimes.htm).

22. Robert C. Shaler, *Who They Were* (New York: Free Press, 2005), p. 295; John Barbanel, "Remains of Unidentified 9/11 Victims Moved to World Trade Center Site," *Wall Street Journal*, May 10, 2014.

23. Stephen Ferrell, "In 'Ceremonial Transfer,' Remains of 9/11 Victims Are Moved to Memorial," *New York Times*, May 10, 2014 (www.nytimes.com /2014/05/11/nyregion/remains-of-9-11-victims-are-transferred-to-trade -center-site.html).

24. Shaler, *Who They Were*, pp. 204–08; N. R. Kleinfield, "Error Put Body of One Firefighter in Grave of a Firehouse Colleague," *New York Times*, November 28, 2001 (www.nytimes.com/2001/11/28/nyregion/nation-challenged -remains-error-put-body-one-firefighter-grave-firehouse.html).

25. Peter Bill, Pavel L. Ivanov, et al., "Identification of the Remains of the Romanov Family by DNA Analysis," *Nature Genetics* 6 (1994), pp. 130–35.

26. Michael D. Coble, "Y-STRs, mtDNA, and the Romanov Case," National Institute of Standards and Technology, April 18, 2012 (www.cstl .nist.gov/strbase/training/NY-Apr2012-Y-mtDNA-Romanovs-handout .pdf).

27. Bruce S. Weir, "The Rarity of DNA Profiles," *Annals of Applied Statistics* 1 (2007), pp. 358–70 (www.ncbi.nlm.nih.gov/pmc/articles/PMC258 5748/).

28. Kathryn Troyer, Theresa Gilboy, and Brian Koeneman, "A Nine STR Locus Match between Two Apparently Unrelated Individuals Using Amp-FISTR Profiler Plus and Cofiler," *Proceedings of the Promega 12th International Symposium on Human Identification* (2001) (www.promega.com/~/media/files /resources/conference%20proceedings/ishi%2012/poster%20abstracts /troyer.pdf).

29. Weir, "The Rarity of DNA Profiles."

30. Jason Felch and Maura Dolan, "Crime Labs Finding Questionable DNA Matches," SFGate.com, August 3, 2008 (www.sfgate.com/news/article /Crime-labs-finding-questionable-DNA-matches-3274788.php#page-1).

31. Persi Diaconis and Frederick Mosteller, "Methods for Studying Co-incidences," *Journal of the American Statistical Association* 84, no. 408 (1989), pp. 853–61.

32. Weir, "The Rarity of DNA Profiles."

33. Nassim Nicholas Taleb, *The Black Swan: The Impact of the Highly Im-probable* (New York: Random House, 2007).

34. FBI, "Face Recognition" (www.fbi.gov/about-us/cjis/fingerprints _biometrics/biometric-center-of-excellence/files/face-recognition.pdf).

35. National Institutes of Health, "What Was the Human Genome Proj-ect and Why Has It Been Important?" (http://ghr.nlm.nih.gov/handbook /hgp/description).

36. "Rapist Convicted on DNA Match," *New York Times*, February 6, 1988 (www.nytimes.com/1988/02/06/us/rapist-convicted-on-dna-match .html).

37. Pat Morrison, "Barry Scheck on the O. J. Trial, DNA Evidence and the Innocence Project," *Los Angeles Times*, June 17, 2014 (www.latimes.com /opinion/op-ed/la-oe-0618-morrison-scheck-oj-simpson-20140618 -column.html#page=1).

38. Graham Rayman, "The NYPD Tapes: Inside Bed-Stuy's 81st Pre-cinct," *Village Voice*, May 4, 2010 (www.villagevoice.com/2010-05-04/news /the-nypd-tapes-inside-bed-stuy-s-81st-precinct/).

39. Ibid.

40. John A. Eterno and Eli B. Silverman, *The Crime Numbers Game: Man-agement by Manipulation* (Hoboken, N.J.: CRC Press, 2012).

41. John A. Eterno and Eli B. Silverman, "NYPD Crime Stats Manipu-lation Widespread, Must Be Investigated, Criminologists Say," *Village Voice*, March 7, 2012 (http://blogs.villagevoice.com/runninscared/2012/03/nypd _crime_stat_1.php).

42. William Bratton, "Crime by the Numbers," *New York Times*, Febru-ary 17, 2010 (http://goo.gl/zOUXrZ). For a broader look at the cross-pressures in performance management, see Donald P. Moynihan, *The Dynamics of Performance Management: Construction Information and Reform* (Georgetown

University Press, 2008); Robert D. Behn, *The PerformanceStat Potential: A Leadership Strategy for Producing Results* (Brookings, 2014).

43. Julie Creswell and Reed Abelson, "Hospital Chain Said to Scheme to Inflate Bills," *New York Times*, January 23, 2014 (www.nytimes.com/2014/01 /24/business/hospital-chain-said-to-scheme-to-inflate-bills.html?hp&_r=0).

44. David A. Fahrenthold, "How the VA Developed Its Culture of Cover-erups," *Washington Post*, May 30, 2014 (www.washingtonpost.com/sf/national /2014/05/30/how-the-va-developed-its-culture-of-coverups/).

45. Charles E. Lindblom and David K. Cohen, *Usable Knowledge: Social Science and Social Problem Solving* (Yale University Press, 1979), p. 1. See also Carol H. Weiss, *Using Social Research for Public Policy Making* (Lexington, Mass.: D.C. Heath & Co., 1977).

46. Francis Fukuyama, *Political Order and Political Decay: From the Industrial Revolution to the Globalization of Democracy* (New York: Farrar, Straus, and Giroux, 2014), pp. 521–22.

47. See Laura Haynes, Owain Service, Ben Goldacre, and David Torgerson, *Test, Learn, Adapt: Developing Public Policy with Randomised Controlled Trials* (London: Cabinet Office, 2012), p. 4 (www.gov.uk/government/publications /test-learn-adapt-developing-public-policy-with-randomised-controlled -trials). See also Pew-MacArthur Results First Initiative, *Evidence-Based Policymaking: A Guide for Effective Government* (Washington, D.C., 2014) (https:// docs.google.com/viewer?url=http%3A%2F%2Fwww.pewtrusts.org%2F ~%2Fmedia%2FAssets%2F2014%2F11%2FEvidenceBasedPolicymakingA GuideforEffectiveGovernment.pdf%3Fla%3Den).

48. Robert D. Behn, "The Black Box of Randomized Controlled Trials," *Performance Leadership Report*, January 2015 (www.hks.harvard.edu /thebehnreport/All%20Issues/BehnReport%202015Jan.pdf), emphasis in the original. More generally, see Behn, *The PerformanceStat Potential*.

49. City of Chicago, "311 Frequently Asked Questions" (2015) (www .cityofchicago.org/city/en/depts/311/supp_info/faq.html).

50. "311 GIS" (https://311gis.com).

51. Montgomery County, Md., "MCDOT Storm Operations" (www7 .montgomerycountymd.gov/snowmap/).

52. National Academy of Public Administration, *Anticipating the Future: Developing a Vision and Strategic Plan for the Social Security Administration for*

2025–2030 (Washington, D.C.: NAPA, 2014) (www.napawash.org/images /reports/2014/2014_AnticipatingTheFutureSSA.pdf).

53. Code for America, "Adopt-A-Hydrant" (www.codeforamerica.org /apps/adopt-a-hydrant/).

54. AccuWeather.com, "Adopt a Hydrant: How a Social App Changed Snowstorm Response" (January 29, 2015) (www.accuweather.com/en/weather -news/adopt-a-hydrant-snowstorms/19897879).

CHAPTER SEVEN

1. iScream Works, since closed (www.yelp.com/biz/iscream-works-west -roxbury).

2. Evan Allen and Todd Feathers, "West Roxbury Couple Charged in Ponzi Scheme," BostonGlobe.com, March 18, 2013 (https://www.bostonglobe .com/metro/2013/03/18/roxbury-couple-charged-with-multi-million -dollar-ponzi-scheme/5ab26g6fC8VHPCSItWvjtL/story.html).

3. Andy Medici, "Senator Asks Kids Directly: Do You Want to Be a Fed?" *Federal Times*, May 22, 2015 (www.federaltimes.com/story/government /management/oversight/2015/05/22/federal-service/27772685/).

4. Evan Allen, "Boston Pair Alleged to Take Millions in Ponzi Scheme," BostonGlobe.com, March 19, 2013 (www.bostonglobe.com/metro/2013/03 /18/west-roxbury-couple-charged-with-multi-million-dollar-ponzi -scheme/3hNV2UR0wicmsuO3YemvGN/story.html).

5. Josh Israel, "31 Senate Republicans Opposed Sandy Relief after Sup- porting Disaster Aid for Home States," ThinkProgress.com, January 29, 2013 (http://thinkprogress.org/economy/2013/01/29/1510041/sandy-aid-re publican-hypocrites/).

6. Jeffrey Tryens, "Using Indicators to Engage Citizens: The Oregon Progress Board Experience," presented at OECD World Forum on Key In- dicators: Statistics, Knowledge and Policy, Palermo, November 10–13, 2004 (www.oecd.org/site/worldforum/33832894.doc).

7. Robert D. Behn, *The PerformanceStat Potential: A Leadership Strategy for Producing Results* (Brookings, 2014).

8. Office of Information and Regulatory Affairs, Office of Management and Budget, *Information Collection Budget of the United States Government: 2014*

(2014) (www.whitehouse.gov/sites/default/files/omb/inforeg/icb/icb_2014
.pdf).

9. John Bridgeland and Peter Orszag, "Can Government Play Moneyball?" *Atlantic* (July/August 2013) (www.theatlantic.com/magazine/archive
/2013/07/can-government-play-moneyball/309389/).

10. Anthony Petrosino, Carolyn Turpin-Petrosino, and James O. Finck-
enauer, "Well-Meaning Programs Can Have Harmful Effects! Lessons from
Experiments of Programs Such as Scared Straight," *Crime and Delinquency*
46, no. 3 (2000), pp. 354–379.

11. Dan Balz, "A GOP Governor Not Running for President Has Ideas
for Politicians Who Are," WashingtonPost.com, March 28, 2015 (www
.washingtonpost.com/politics/a-gop-governor-not-running-for-president
-has-ideas-for-those-who-are/2015/03/28/a443795c-d4c8-11e4-8fce
-3941fc548f1c_story.html).

12. John J. DiIulio Jr., *Bring Back the Bureaucrats* (West Conshohocken,
Pa.: Templeton Press, 2014).

13. Charles Murray, "No Cure for the Sclerotic State," in ibid., p. 123.

14. POGO, "Feds vs. Contractors: Federal Employees Often Save Money,
but an Advisory Panel Is Needed to Create a Cost Comparison Model,"
April 15, 2013 (www.pogo.org/our-work/letters/2013/20130415-feds-vs
-contractors-cost-comparison.html); POGO, *Bad Business: Billions of Taxpayer Dollars Wasted on Hiring Contractors*, September 13, 2011 (www.pogo
.org/our-work/reports/2011/co-gp-20110913.html).

15. Dana Priest and William M. Arkin, "National Security Inc.," *Washington Post*, July 20, 2010 (http://projects.washingtonpost.com/top-secret
-america/articles/national-security-inc/print/).

16. David Berteau et al., *DOD Workforce Cost Realism Assessment*
(Washington, D.C.: Center for Strategic and International Studies, 2011),
http://csis.org/files/publication/110517_Berteau_DoDWorkforceCost
_Web.pdf.

17. U.S. Government Accountability Office, *Human Capital: Opportunities Exist to Further Improve DOD's Methodology for Estimating the Costs of Its
Workforces*, GAO-13-792, September 2013 (www.gao.gov/assets/660/658131
.pdf).

18. David Osborne and Ted Gaebler, *Reinventing Government: How the Entrepreneurial Spirit Is Transforming the Public Sector* (New York: Plume, 1993).

19. Teresa Derrick-Mills, Mary K. Winkler, Olivia Healy, and Erica Greenberg, *A Resource Guide for Head Start Programs: Moving beyond a Culture of Compliance to a Culture of Continuous Improvement* (Washington, D.C.: Urban Institute, 2015) (www.urban.org/sites/default/files/alfresco/publication -pdfs/2000185-Moving-Beyond-a-Culture-of-Compliance-to-a-Culture -of-Continuous-Improvement.pdf).

20. Michele Jolin, "Preface," in Jim Nuzzle and Peter Orszag, *Moneyball for Government* (Washington, D.C.: Disruption Books, 2014), pp. vii–viii.

21. Whit Ayres, *2016 and Beyond: How Republicans Can Elect a President in the New America* (Washington, D.C.: Resurgent Republic, 2015), p. 41.

22. Ibid., p. 53.

23. Pew Research Center, "As Sequester Deadline Looms, Little Support for Cutting Most Programs," February 22, 2013 (www.people-press.org/2013 /02/22/as-sequester-deadline-looms-little-support-for-cutting-most -programs/).

24. White House, "Making Open and Machine Readable the New Default for Government Information," May 9, 2013 (www.whitehouse.gov /the-press-office/2013/05/09/executive-order-making-open-and-machine -readable-new-default-government-).

25. Khristina Narizhnaya and Lia Eustachewich, "This Couple Has the Loudest Sex in NYC," NewYorkPost.com, April 23, 2015 (http://nypost.com /2015/04/23/meet-new-york-citys-loudest-lovers-according-to-311-calls/).

26. Matthew Flamm, "City's 311 Hotline Is Getting Some Help of Its Own," *Crain's New York Business*, April 30, 2015 (www.crainsnewyork.com /article/20150430/TECHNOLOGY/150429832/citys-311-hotline-is -getting-some-help-of-its-own).

27. "New York Health Department Restaurant Ratings Map," New YorkTimes.com (www.nytimes.com/interactive/dining/new-york-health -department-restaurant-ratings-map.html).

28. *Restaurant Grading in New York City at 18 Months: Public Recognition and Use of Grades—Trends in Restaurant Sanitary Conditions and Foodborne Illnesses* (New York: New York City Health Department, undated) (www.nyc

.gov/html/doh/downloads/pdf/rii/restaurant-grading-18-month-report
.pdf).

29. Hallie Golden, "Why Americans Don't Trust the Government to Safeguard Their Data," NextGov.com, July 2, 2015 (www.nextgov.com /cybersecurity/2015/07/do-consumers-trust-agencies-their-personal -information/116848/); "Survey: Most Americans Just Not That into Uncle Sam's Digital Service," NextGov.com, April 28, 2015 (www.nextgov.com/cio -briefing/2015/04/adults-are-just-not-federal-digital-services/111292/).

30. Quoted by Michael Grass, "A Municipal Innovation Priority: People Want Information and 'They Want It Now,'" *Route 50* (Government Executive, May 21, 2015) (www.routefifty.com/2015/05/philadelphia-311-innovation /113458/).

Chapter Eight

1. Alexander Pope, *An Essay on Man*, epistle 3, lines 302–03 (www.bartleby .com/40/2803.html).

2. Xi Jinping, "Study for a Brighter Future," March 1, 2013, in *The Governance of China* (Beijing: Foreign Languages Press, 2014), p. 449.

3. "Platform of the Progressive Party," August 7, 1912 (www.pbs.org /wgbh/americanexperience/features/primary-resources/tr-progressive/).

4. Archon Fong, "Infotopia: Unleashing the Democratic Power of Transparency," *Politics and Society* 41 (2013), pp. 208–09.

5. Ibid., p. 209.

6. On the use of sophisticated benefit-cost analysis, see the Pew-MacArthur Results First Initiative (www.pewtrusts.org/en/projects/pew -macarthur-results-first-initiative); on performance management, see Robert D. Behn, *The PerformanceStat Potential* (Brookings, 2014).

7. Josh Hicks, "House Republicans Propose Shrinking Federal Workforce, Cutting Service Contracts," *Washington Post*, January 23, 2015 (www .washingtonpost.com/blogs/federal-eye/wp/2015/01/23/house-republicans -propose-shrinking-federal-workforce-cutting-service-contracts/).

8. U.S. Government Accountability Office, "Improving the Management of IT Acquisitions and Operations," 2015 (www.gao.gov/highrisk/improving _management_it_acquisitions_operations/why_did_study).

9. Craig Timberg, "The Flaw in the Design," *Washington Post*, May 30, 2015 (www.washingtonpost.com/sf/business/2015/05/30/net-of-insecurity -part-1/).

10. Craig Timberg and Ellen Nakashima, "Government Computers Running Windows XP Will Be Vulnerable to Hackers after April 8," *Washington Post*, March 16, 2014 (www.washingtonpost.com/business/technology /government-computers-running-windows-xp-will-be-vulnerable-to -hackers-after-april-8/2014/03/16/9a9c8c7c-a553-11e3-a5fa-55f0c77bf39c _story.html).

Index